ANTHROPOS.

BY THE

REV. W. P. BREED, D.D.

AUTHOR OF

"MAN RESPONSIBLE FOR HIS BELIEF," &c.

"ON EARTH THERE'S NOTHING GREAT BUT MAN."

PHILADELPHIA:
PRESBYTERIAN BOARD OF PUBLICATION,
No. 821 CHESTNUT STREET.

STEREOTYPED BY WESTCOTT & THOMSON.

CONTENTS.

ANTHROPOS.

I.

ANTHROPOS.

"While the mute creation downward bend
Their gaze, and to their earthly mother tend,
Man looks aloft, and with erected eyes
Beholds his own hereditary skies."

THE Greek word anthropos is given us in the lexicons as a triple compound, made up first, of an adverb that signifies "upward;" then of the fragment of a verb that means "to turn," and lastly of a noun that designates the "human face." The whole, combined in one word, points us to man as the creature that turns his face toward the skies.

In this term we may find a reference either to that peculiarity of physical structure that makes an upward look possible, natural, and easy to man, or to a real or supposed yearning in human nature for a higher destiny, or to that sense of dependence upon a higher power that has so abundantly and variously expressed itself in man's religious history, teaching him to look for help from above, or to all of these together. And it is not impossible that there may lurk within it a hint as to human duty to the powers supposed to reign on high.

However this may be, it is an interesting fact, that man is furnished with a singular and beautiful combination of joints in the neck, at the top of the spinal column—a ball and socket joint, enabling him to turn the face from side to side, and a hinge joint permitting him at will to throw back the head, and gaze into the heavens. Thus he is, in his physical structure, an anthropos, a looker toward the skies.

II.

MAN.

"What am I? Whence produced, and for what end?
Am I the abandoned orphan of blind chance,
Dropped by wild atoms in disordered dance?
Or from an endless chain of causes wrought,
And of unthinking substance, born with thought.
Am I but what I am, mere flesh and blood,
A branching channel, with a mazy flood?"

MANY have been the definitions given of man, some sportive and some grave. He has been called an unfeathered bird—a food-cooking, fire-using animal—the talking animal, the animal that laughs and weeps—an animal capable of acquiring knowledge. Strict materialism defines him a thinking organism, an animal whose organs secrete thought.

But whatever else is true or untrue of man, it is certain that he is distinguished from all other terrestrial beings by the power of self-knowledge.

He possesses self-consciousness. He is intelligently aware of his own existence, of the thoughts arising, and the emotions that play within him, and of the motives that impel him to action.

The eye that sees other objects cannot see itself, but man is an eye that can see himself.

"The stars that shine, and the planets that
Wheel unshaken in the wide universe,"

the winds that whisper in the summer evening, and howl in the winter tempest, the ocean now a smooth mirror, reflecting back the glory of the skies, and now raging under the torment of the storm, and all birds, beasts, fishes and insects, all execute the will of God, and perform the parts severally assigned them in the economy of nature, and help to weave the wondrous web of human history, and yet all as incapable of truly knowing that they exist, and what they are, and what they do, as the loom that weaves its ingenious tapestries, or the printing press that embalms upon the paper page the thoughts of a Homer, Milton or Bacon. But man, among all these the only true actor in human affairs, is a self-conscious being, and knows not only that he is, but to a large extent what he is and what he does.

Doubtless there lie hidden in the recesses of his nature, mysteries too deep to be reached by any sounding line as yet in his possession. And his influence is more impressive and far-reaching than he often suspects, or is able to comprehend.

Still he is an eye that sees himself—a loom that may know to a large extent what he weaves, a printing press that is conscious of the thoughts that he imprints upon the page of his own and the world's records.

The mere animal has its instincts that feebly and but feebly typify the mental processes of man, though they enable it to achieve results that fill us with surprise and admiration. With the nest of the bird, the web of the spider, the cell of the bee, the architecture and strange economies and wars of the ant, we are all more or less familiar. Through the operations of this mimic intelligence, we are told that "the ox eats two hundred and seventy-six herbs, but rejects two hundred and eighteen; that the goat finds four hundred and forty-nine palatable, but feels averse to one hundred and twenty-seven; the sheep three hundred and eighty-seven, not touching one hundred and forty-one; the horse two hundred and sixty-two, leaving two hundred and twelve untasted. The reindeer lays itself down, scrapes away the deep snow with its horn and fore-feet, and finds its aliment."

This animal instinct is a matter of profound interest, and has given exercise to some of the acutest of philosophical minds. Descartes discussed it, and Lord Brougham has a charming little volume upon it. But whatever may be the general truth respecting its nature, it is without all doubt as nothing to the commanding intellect of man.

He, too, has his instincts, but they are at the bidding of his higher powers. Shatter the leg of a lion, and he will howl in dismay and despair. "But when a cannon ball fell into the room of Charles the XII., and he remained calmly in his chair—when the Dutch Admiral, in the moment he was to take a pinch of snuff, and lost the extended hand by a shot, took it with the other—and when the British cannonier, whose right hand was torn off by a ball as he was about to discharge his cannon, used the left with the words, "Does the enemy think that I have but one hand?"—they showed, as President Rauch in his Psychology well remarks, "That they by their will were above the necessity of yielding to fear, or the influence of pain.

Man then is an animal, or rather he possesses and may use an animal nature, with all its array of appetites and instincts, but the possessor of these is something vastly higher and nobler than the animal nature possessed.

And one of the grandest of his attributes is the power to know himself. He may dissect the body, count and study the bones, muscles and sinews that make up this strange life-bundle. He may, to a large extent, fathom the physiological wonders that are hinged together in a marvellous system of harmonious action and reaction, in health, disease, growth and decay. And he may go down into the chambers of his own mind, and there setting himself before himself, he may become at once the observer and the observed, in its constitution and action.

It is possible, it is not uncommon, to become so engrossed with the remote, as to overlook and neglect what is nearest. Many a man can tell about bees and ants, while yet he knows little or nothing about himself. One in gazing at the stars may walk off a precipice and perish.

We propose a brief survey of some of the strange things embosomed in our nature, and to consider some of the solemnities, responsibilities and possibilities involved therein.

III.

MAN TO MEN.

"Man is one:
And he hath one great heart. It is thus we feel,
With a gigantic throb athwart the sea,
Each other's rights and wrongs; thus are we men."

MANY centuries ago, the great Aristotle wrote, "Man to man is the most attractive of all objects." And it may justify and help to persuade to self-inspection and study, to glance at this truth and some of its illustrations.

Is it not true that man merits and actually occupies a very high place in human regards?

Gather the works upon which man has poured his loftiest and most ardent and brilliant thinkings, and see to how large an extent his brother man has engrossed them. The painter who paints, and the sculptor who moulds, not for the present hour but for human interest during all coming time, take care to give man a central place in their creations.

And the great epics, that pass the fiery ordeal of the centuries, take their text, and imbue their commentaries with gatherings from the same repository.

Bishop Warburton, in that amazing thesaurus of learning, the "Divine Legation," insists, that human literature has room but for three true epic poems, and assigns the occupancy of this literary realm to that royal triumvirate, Homer, Virgil and Milton. The first possessed himself of the province of morality, the second that of politics, and the last that of religion. "These are the three species of the epic poem; for its largest sphere is human action, which can only be considered in a moral, political and religious view."

There remains, however, another grand sphere of literary labour, which, however, embraces all the themes of all these three, and that is History. And Herodotus, and Thucydides, and Gibbon and Macaulay will still hold their places in human libraries, side by side with Warburton's grand triumvirate. And the charm that secures them their immortality grows out of man's interest in men. And the historic page, whatever other claim it may have to human regard, needs no other than the fact that it frowns or smiles, weeps or bleeds with the crimes, virtues, struggles, darings, victories, defeats, joys and woes of our kind!

It is these that hallow the scenes where they have taken place.

"What's hallowed ground?
A kiss can consecrate the ground
Where mated heads are mutual bound;
The spot where love's first links are wound,
That never are riven,
Is hallowed down to earth's profound,
And up to heaven."

And if a kiss, much more a tear. And if a tear, much more a drop of blood. And what is human history but a long tale of tear-shedding and blood-shedding?

Indeed let a man but once cross your pathway in human life—let him be thrown together with you for but the casual intercourse of a single hour, and a greater or less interest is thereby awakened in your heart in his behalf. And years after, if tidings reach you of that stranger as the sharer in some strange good fortune, or the victim of some bloody outrage, or the subject of some sore calamity, that past acquaintance of an hour, now recalled, will invest the tidings with a tenfold interest in your mind and heart.

To the traveller in remote and unfrequented regions, though nature may concentrate about him her beauties and sublimities, yet if in the midst of all, a man emerge to view, his heart will thrill with an intensity of fresh delight.

Our western plains are diversified with certain excavations and upthrowings of earth, which, as mere terrestrial elevations and depressions, lack all special claim to human regard. Yet in fact they have attracted man in solitary pilgrimage and in caravans, to inspect and gaze with mysterious awe upon them.

Why now this pre-eminence accorded to them in man's regards over many a mass of terrestrial sublimity of God's own workmanshp? The secret lies here. Those mysterious mounds bear indisputable evidence that minds have thought and hands have wrought them—hands and minds of our brethren according to the flesh, of whose career and doom, history, tradition and song are alike silent as the grave, and of whom the only tidings within human reach are the enigmatical whisperings of those fast decaying earthworks.

The geologist, as he turns over leaf after leaf of that rocky volume in which nature has been so long writing her autobiography, no matter how deep his interest in the fossil remains of vast ungainly monsters, of fern-prints and fish turned to stone, all is forgotten if the foot-prints of a fellow-man come to view.

And yonder landscape, of hill and dale, of winding stream with flowery banks, of tall trees and lesser shrubs, villages in the distance, and flocks browsing in the meadows—is it beautiful? Does it surpass all actual art, and mock conception of improvement? Well, if man cannot excell it upon the canvass in lines and colours, he still has his triumph. He is able to invest even that, or any other scene in nature, with a vastly enhanced interest over the human heart. While engrossed with its natural beauties, let some one whisper in your ear,

"In yonder grove, Pocahontas saved the life of Smith. Beneath yonder spreading elm, Penn made his treaty with the Indians. On yonder plain the mailed knights of England extorted from their lackland king the Magna Charta. In yonder house, Milton was born—in that one, Shakspeare died. Yonder rock received the foot of Tell, as he sprang from the grasp of Gesler. Yonder field, where now the nodding corn invites the sickle, when the sun of Waterloo went down, was 'covered thick with other clay—'

> "Heaped and pent,
> Rider and horse, friend and foe, in one red burial blent.'"

Nay, even at Niagara, where that world of waters rushes in tumultuous merriment down that awful hill, and then, wreathing its brow with rainbows, plunges into the wild abyss, well assured that he who bids the leap will know where to find every precious drop—even there, we say, if pointed to the spot whence slipped the maiden, to rescue whom her lover sprang and both were swept to death—Niagara herself, present with us face to face, vanishes from our apprehension!

In a word, let physical nature do her utmost; let her exhaust all her treasures of beauty and sublimity to throw a spell over the human spirit, and then, but let that scene become associated with the doings and darings, the triumphs or the woes of man, our brother, and the spectator's bosom will heave with a tumult of emotions that nothing else could possibly evoke. Niagara's voice is drowned to silence in that one maiden's shriek. Niagara's glories are eclipsed to darkness by the woe of that one hapless youth!

So genuine, so general and intense is the interest, that man awakens in the bosom of his brother man! Why, then, should he not seek acquaintance with himself?

IV.

MAN IN THE BIBLE.

"THE word of God, as contained in the Scriptures of the Old and New Testaments," is mostly conceived of by men as a revelation of which God is the chief subject, as well as the author. We are, perhaps, too much in the habit of considering it as the all-engrossing aim and end of holy writ to remove the veil that hides the attributes of the Divine Being, and make him better known.

But it merits attention also, that in so far as God is the theme of inspiration, men are the audience addressed therein, and that it was in order that his glory might shine through men, that the Holy Spirit brooded over the sacred penmen, furnishing matter, and so controlling the mind as to secure an infallible and authoritative record of the Divine will.

But in truth, the Bible is hardly more an unveiling of God than it is of man; and a chief aim, and one grand result of inspired teaching, is to make man known to himself.

And, indeed, a theology of any practical value is impossible, unless coupled with a sound anthropology.

Beyond the reach of the rays of revelation, all know how wild have been the anthropologies of even the sages of the highest civilizations. Thales, the father of Greek philosophies, was to himself, in nature, origin and destiny, a profound mystery. Nor did the oscillations of philosophic speculation, for two centuries from his time to Socrates and Plato, develope truth for a single sound and reliable proposition upon this subject. And the teachings and progress of four centuries more left that noble inquirer, Cicero, still in the dark, as to whether there dwelt within him a soul that would survive the shock of death that laid the body in the grave. No one can follow him in his dark gropings after the truth among the masses of contradictory opinion without a deep commiseration for his perplexities, nor read, but with a pang, the touching confession he puts into the mouth of one of the interlocutors in his discussions of the nature of the soul.

"I know not how it is, but while I am reading Plato, I feel fully assured of the soul's immortality; but when I lay aside his book, all my firmness of assurance passes away."

If this were so with the cultivated and acute Greek and Roman mind, we need not wonder at the marvellous visions that have haunted the thoughts of the imaginative Orientals.

Brahm wakes from his long slumber and becomes Brahma; and out of Brahm matter issues, and these latter united form the universe. This universe contains mind, and the grosser elements, and the union of these produces the genii and men. Then comes the endless series of transmigrations, the aim of which, through aid of religion, is the reabsorption of the individual into the great soul.

Connected with this is that masterpiece of Satan, Caste. From Brahma's head come the Brahmins, the predestinated masters of mankind. From other parts of the god, the other classes issue, down to the foot, whence come the poor Indras. These, with their thirty or forty subdivisions, constitute a social system which forms one of the most formidable barriers that true religion is called to surmount.

Thus, our missionaries can gain no access for the truth but by breaching these walls and overthrowing to its foundations this monstrous anthropology.

Hence, the opening page of revelation tells the true story of man's origin and nature. A personal God creates him in his own image. Matter is moulded, with exquisite workmanship, into a most beautiful form, and into this form God breathes a life, and man becomes a living soul.

As the opening page of God's book tells how man came into being, an early record shows how he fell, and furnishes us with the explanation of the physical ills and moral perturbations which fill the earth with disorder, and cover it with the pall of death.

Then comes the gradual development of the scheme for his redemption and rescue. Altar-fires begin to blaze, and altars and sacrifices to be multiplied. Abraham is called. Moses is rescued from the Nile and builds the tabernacle. Solomon erects the temple. In the fulness of time Christ comes, the Lamb of God, to take away the sins of the world. Faith lights her torch; hope holds out her star; and man, by aid of the cross, climbs back to heights that Adam in paradise never knew.

And from beginning to end of the Holy Word, man constantly appears as the chief actor in its scenes, and the chief object of its provisions. If devils come upon the stage, their aim is to ruin man. If angelic interventions abound, their object is sometimes to execute judgments upon, but oftener to lend a helping hand to man. "Are they not *all* ministering spirits sent forth to minister for them who shall be heirs of salvation?"

In these pages, man's character is powerfully, terribly delineated; "deceitful above all things, desperately wicked; abominable, filthy, drinking in iniquity, like water."

His condition before God is displayed; under condemnation, by nature, "a child of wrath." His duty is declared. Appeals, warnings, exhortations, expostulations, threats, and invitations abound.

And the volume closes with pictures; some grand, some terrible as imagination ever conceived, of the two several abodes into one or other of which man passes when hidden from earthly scenes.

Thus, if this book is all alive with God, it is not less alive with man.

The one hundred and thirty-ninth psalm may be taken in this respect as a kind of epitome of the whole book. There we find these two grand subjects of inspired teaching coupled in some of the sublimest strains of David's minstrelsy. The psalm opens with the two in juxtaposition, man under the burning eye of God. "O Lord, thou hast searched me, and known me!"

In the sentences next following, this general truth is reduced to particulars. In every posture and position, in all his ways, going and returning, rising up and lying down, he is still the object of the divine observation. In this knowledge, the movements of the tongue and the exercises of the mind are included.

"My thoughts, before they are my own,
Are to my God distinctly known;
He knows the words I mean to speak,
Ere from my opening lips they break.

"Within thy circling power I stand,
On every side I find thy hand;
Awake, asleep, at home, abroad,
I am surrounded still with God."

Then follows a brilliant flash of poetic fire, the theme of which is the divine Omnipresence.

"Whither shall I go from thy Spirit? or whither shall I flee from thy presence? If I ascend up into heaven, thou art there; if I make my bed in hell, behold, thou art there! If I take the wings of the morning, and dwell in the uttermost parts of the sea;

even there shall thy hand lead me, and thy right hand shall hold me! If I say, Surely the darkness shall cover me; even the night shall be light about me. Yea, the darkness hideth not from thee; but the night shineth as the day: The darkness and the light are both alike to thee!"

Then, man becomes again the prominent object of thought.

"I will praise thee, for I am fearfully and wonderfully made. My substance was not hid from thee when I was curiously wrought in the lowest parts of the earth. Thine eyes did see my substance, yet being unperfect; and in thy book all my numbers were written, which in continuance, were fashioned, when as yet there was none of them."

If, then, the God of heaven has made man a chief theme of the only written revelation ever penned, well may man make himself the theme of frequent and solemn meditation and study.

V.

MAN TO HIMSELF.

"The proper study of mankind is man."

THE well-known precept, "Know thyself," is said to have been inscribed over the door of Apollo's temple, at Delphi. And if subordinate nature, animate and inanimate, are worthy of study, surely the student himself is not less worthy.

For man's views of his own nature, correct or erroneous, cannot fail to exert important influence upon his conduct, and his conduct sows the seed of a harvest he will spend an eternity in reaping.

If one assume with some philosophers that man is a mere mass of finely organized matter, a mere bundle of flesh and bones, veins and muscles, he will also assume that the world is a great larder fitted up to gratify human appetite, and that man's chief end is to secure the largest possible number of pleasurable sensations at the smallest possible cost.

But let him realize the truths as to his nature and relationship to his brother man on the one hand, and to his Creator on the other; that made in the image of God, he is immortal, accountable, living, thinking and acting under the unclosed eye of him who will adjudge him to an eternity in correspondence with his character and conduct, that death, lurking at every corner, will usher him a naked soul into the presence of his judge, and the pressure of these high truths must give a tone to his spirit, a loftiness to his aims, and a force to his better purposes, that mere materialism cannot conceive.

There are those who never rise to a higher conception of life and of the world, than that which makes the one a great play-ground, and the other a protracted holiday. What man is, they never trouble themselves to inquire. If he is more than a twittering wren, or a swallow, gliding to and fro in the summer air; a gay butterfly, commissioned to flit from flower to flower on sunny fields, they never make the discovery; and hence they do nothing but trifle from one end of life to the other.

The world cries piteously for aid, but the trifler trifles on. Social and political earthquakes unsettle established order, prostrate ivy-grown customs, and inaugurate new schemes and systems, and he, the while, watches with all-engrossing interest the revolutions of fashion. While others grapple in the struggle for the overthrow of some giant wrong, he sighs or exults over some momentous change in the cut of a vest pattern.

War breaks out, and patriotic furors surge like a deluge through the land, and patriotic hosts, leaving all the endearments of home, "mount barbed steeds"

"To fright the souls of fearful adversaries,"

and he the while "courts an amorous looking-glass."

While others seize the musket, he seizes his cane; while others buckle on the cartridge-box, he buckles on his neck-tie; while others march to battle, he marches up and down the fashionable thoroughfares, a gratuitous advertiser of the wares of the man-dresser.

And at length he reaches the end of his life, (for varieties as well as values have an end,) and looking back through an avenue of forty or fifty years, with widows here and orphans there; here the groping tribes of the indigent blind, and there of the deaf mute; here the poor children of lunacy, and there the populous hospital-ward, and everywhere the poor and ragged and wretched, and what in the name of humanity has he done for them?

And now, what has he to show to his conscience, to society, and to God, for all these years of life's gifts, enjoyments, and opportunities; what but a manly account of so much bread consumed, so many suits of clothing worn out, perhaps so many horses disabled, and carriages defaced, and a respectable pyramid of broken champagne bottles and empty cigar boxes?

And what has he to offer to the grave but a mass of dust that had been more profitably expended in constructing an ox, a horse, or a faithful dog, and what to God but a soul that had better never been created!

One whose name is known to almost every child in the land, when approached upon the great subject of man's destiny, replied, that he cared not to trouble himself now with these matters, for he should soon pass to another world, and then he would know the whole truth without the trouble of inquiring. As if the commandant of a national ship, in time of war, ordered on a cruise, should spend his time as comfortably as he could in his cabin till his provisions ran out, and then return to ask the government whither, and for what he was sent. It will be too late in the life to come first to inquire what one ought to do in this.

But in some instances, at least, the question as to man's nature and destiny will-not suffer itself to be quietly postponed.

Seated in our study one summer evening, the door-bell announced a visitor. He was a youth of perhaps nineteen, of uncommon acuteness and uncommon thoughtfulness of mind. He had come to talk about his soul.

Long and interesting was the conversation that ensued. He evidently thought for himself, and exhibited an almost morbid disregard for authority. He was willing, even anxious to be a Christian, provided he could reason his way through, and be able to give to himself, and especially to others, a rational account of the processes and objects of faith. He was even afraid that his desire to become a Christian would have an undue influence upon his judgment and action in the case.

Some of his views were dreamy and pantheistic in their tone. "I sometimes," he said, "fancy myself a mere dream, destitute of real existence. Mysteries encompass and baffle me. I know not which way to turn."

He, however, avowed that realities he could not permanently doubt, and possibilities that he could neither affirm nor deny were sometimes the occasion of mental disturbance that rose almost to anguish.

"Here I am," he said. "I am not here for ever. Die I must. I may die to-night. What then? Perhaps I shall be annihilated. This I could welcome, but perhaps I shall not. I may survive death; and if so, I may be miserable; I may be happy; but all is involved in doubt."

"I do not believe that there is a God; but I do not believe that there is not. I have no ground on which I can base either proposition. I am all at sea without a rudder or a chart. For all I know there may be a triune God and an atonement, a judgment, a hell and a heaven. I do not know that there is a hell, and yet I know that to-morrow I *may* be there."

"This utter uncertainty makes either happiness or rest impossible. I often lie awake at midnight and cannot and dare not sleep, lest I be launched into the abyss of the unknown."

I anxiously sought for the source of this state of mind so unusual in one so young, and I found that, like many others, he had in his quest for a so-called rational religion thought it needful to study "the other side of the question." He must not, like a child, take his faith from the hand of tradition, but must construct a creed for himself. Hence, he must read what had been written against religion also. And he had read! Read every infidel book that came in his way; and he had so mastered them, that he had come into possession, or rather, he had put himself into the possession of all the doubts and sneers and sarcasms that ribald infidelity had heaped up in its literature. These so swarmed in his mind, that whenever an argument for the truth rose to his thoughts, it was at once cancelled by some ready infidel contradiction, or so crippled, that it could not make its way to his convictions. Thus, by infidel aid, he had disabled his own powers of believing the truth. He was like a poor inebriate, so chained by his awful habits, that although he at times more than suspected that he was destroying his own soul, he was helpless for reform. One sight of the wine-cup would drown all his better resolutions, and take captive all his better judgments.

I asked him to lend me one of his most potent authorities. He sent me one. It was Dr. Hobach's "System of Nature," with foot-notes by Diderot, a rigid and powerfully reasoned system of materialism. He, however, could not see the absurdity of

Diderot's malignant denunciations of those who held opposing creeds; for if the system of material necessity were true, his opponents could no more help believing and acting as they did, than the Mississippi could help flowing, or Niagara falling. Nor could he see that the reasoning of his cherished author was the most vicious of circles. For according to him, all events were a mere series of inevitable causes and effects without any *first cause.* Nature was a great mill with shafts, bands and spindle, without any motive power to set it agoing. There was an adamantine chain of consecutive links, but no staple to hang the chain on!

How thoroughly that book had been studied, however, was manifest from its appearance. And he, poor fellow, was more thoroughly entangled in its coils than were Laocoon and his sons in those of the twin serpent on the shores of Troy.

In his then state of mind, he made me think of the Indian, who, sleeping in his canoe, was imperceptibly wafted out upon Niagara's current, and awakened only by the hissing and howling of the waters on the margin of the precipice. There seemed nothing left for him but to sing his death-song and perish. And from what I have learned of that youth since, I tremble to think that this was indeed his end!

But there are certain things that we may learn of our nature by a little reflection, and to some of these we propose to point the reader's attention.

VI.

MAN AS HE IS.

"Learn more of reverence, not for rank or wealth—that needs no learning;
That comes quickly, quick as sin does! Aye, and often leads to sin.
But for Adam's seed—MAN! Trust me; 'tis a clay above your scorning,
With God's image stamped upon it, and God's kindling breath within."

WE recall the brief pregnant saying, already quoted from the word of God, in which the psalmist writes:

"I am fearfully and wonderfully made."

Perhaps a strictly literal rendering of this passage would read—"With terrible things I am made wonderful." But either rendering classifies the truths respecting our nature under these two general heads—the Fearful and the Wonderful. Now, it is true, that the several topics thus suggested overlap each other. Most of the fearful elements in our nature are wonderful, also, and some of the wonderful are fearful. Yet they are sufficiently distinct to justify a general division of our theme—man as he is—into these two lines of meditation.

Fixing our eye then first on the wonderful, we find it branching into three several streams, each alluring us to a stroll upon its banks. There is first the wonderful, as displayed in our bodily frame; then, the wonderful as seen in our mental or spiritual nature; and last, but by no means least, the wonderful as involved in the union subsisting between these two.

VII.

THE WONDERFUL—THE BODILY FRAME.

The most obvious and palpable among the ele ments of human nature, is the bodily frame. Man is not a body, but he has one. "He is not an organism, but an intelligence served by organs." In general and of right, the man is the master of the body; but in some respects, and in some cases, in a degree no way honourable to him, it is his master. It should serve him, but he often serves it. He ought to make it an instrument in a useful, holy life; it often makes him the slave of sin.

It is through the bodily organs that external nature reaches the soul, and affects not only his comfort, but his disposition and character. No doubt more than man knows, he is at the mercy of meteorological, electrical, and magnetic vicissitudes. Heat and cold determine the forms of especially domestic architecture, and to a considerable degree, man's social habits, and thus very largely his character and disposition.

"Will any one deny," asks Dr. Draper, in his "Intellectual Developement of Europe," "the influence of rainy days on our industrial habits, and on our mental condition, even in a civilized state?" "Meteorology to no little extent influences morals; the instinctive tendency to drunkenness is a function of the latitude."

The stolid Esquimaux, the lively Frenchman, and the grave Englishman, owe their differences very much to the effects of external objects upon human nature.

1. In looking at man, the first thing that strikes the eye is his attitude.

In an assemblage of the lower order of animals, one is not long in discovering which of them is of the seed royal. The lordly lion carries dominion in his very tread; but introduce man among them, and both you and they are struck with his great and evident superiority. He stands erect, they are prone. He looks to heaven, and they to earth; and in his eye there is fire that awes the boldest of them.

In this erect position of the body, man is alone among the tribes that tread the earth; all others, by nature, bend forward and look downward to the dust from which they came, and into which, at death, they descend.

The *quadrumana*, whose general structure most closely approximates that of man, such as the chimpanzee and the ourang-outang, of necessity bend forward, and their long arms are ever ready to act the part of legs in their ungainly locomotion. But the human arm, made for nobler purposes, hangs by the side, while the framework, with its well-adjusted curves, brings the centre of gravity between the feet, and makes him, as has been said above, even physically an anthropos, a looker toward the skies.

The erect position in man is at once a distingishing fact and an impressive sermon. The earth beneath his feet is to him but a stepping-stone to something higher, and intimates an upward tendency—an eagle's flight. "They that wait upon the Lord," with eyes turned towards his throne, "shall mount up with wings as eagles; they shall run and not be weary; and they shall walk and not faint."

That earth must remain where God placed it, beneath his feet. It may not climb, with its boasted treasures, into his affections, dragging him down like a wretched muckrake, to dig and scrape in its mire for his chief good. And when licentiousness and drunkenness bend his noble form into similitude with that of the brutes, he exchanges the nature God gave him for a baser, and no longer an anthropos, an upward looker, he becomes a burrower among defilements that unman him, and depravities that debase him.

2. Then the *structure* of the human frame is full of marvels.

The steam engine is properly considered one of the most masterly achievements of human genius. How admirable is that combination of strong arms, cranks, wheels, pistons, and cylinders. The very type of resistless energy, almost of self-acting intelligence; but compared with man, its maker, what is it that thou art mindful of it?

There are those more than two hundred bones, shielding the brain, protecting the eye, forming a sheath for the life-marrow in the spinal column, and in the legs supporting the frame, as "pillars of marble set upon sockets of fine gold," the whole forming firm framework for the system, made up of materials conveyed mysteriously to their places by a series of wonder-working organs.

And how marvellously are these bones combined; some with serrated edges in close suture, as with the bones of the skull; some as the teeth rigidly secure, "like pegs driven into a board;" while others are adapted to the free motions required in the exigencies of life. The ribs projecting forward and downward, by their evolution in respiration open a cavity within large enough to admit from seventy to an hundred cubic inches of air. Nor can any mechanism be more perfect than that displayed in the joints; now a hinge where motion in a single plane is required, as at the knee, and now the ball adjusted to its socket, where a circular motion is needed. In all these cases, too, the tips of the bones are supplied in their delicateness of structure with connecting ligaments and separating pads, and withal a constant supply of lubricating mucilage, preventing friction and rendering action easy and painless.

We need only to add the durability of this machinery of locomotion. "A limb shall swing upon its hinge, or play in its socket many hundred times an hour for sixty years together, without diminution of its agility." Surely we are wonderfully made!

Then, what wonders lie embosomed in that system of muscles, more than five hundred in number, that wrap this long framework round in a covering of flesh with their strange power of contraction and relaxation! Each muscle is a bundle of fibrous cords, and we are told that at least ten several conditions are met in each mass, figure, magnitude, fulcrum, point of action, collocation with respect to the two ends, place, position of the whole muscle and introduction into it of nerves, arteries and veins.

With reference to the joints, the muscles are so adjusted as to work just the effect needed in each case, whether motion in a plane or in a circle. Sometimes they are located at the point where the result is needed; but when this would be inconvenient, as in the fingers, they are placed at a distance and the force conveyed to the proper place by cords strong enough for the purpose, and yet not too large for convenience.

The rapidity of their action is another marvel, as in speaking or playing upon a musical instrument; and another still, is their amazing complication, a hundred of them acting in every breath we draw.

Attention, too, is often called to their interdependence, the failure of a single one of the multitude plunging the subject into suffering.

We are told of one, who, from the failure of two little muscles to act, was long unable to see, except as he lifted his eyelids with his fingers.

> "Our life contains a thousand springs,
> And dies if one be gone;
> Strange, that a harp of thousand strings
> Should keep in tune so long!"

Another world of wonders is disclosed in the nervous system, with its larger masses in the brain and spinal column, its curious ganglion knots, and its endless ramifications through the frame, playing so important a part among the functions of the animal life, and with their inexplicable connections with the mind. So profuse are their radiations from the great centres, and so complicated the mazy net-work with which they overspread the surface of the body, that the finest needle-point can find no room for entrance between them. From millions of minute points these fibrous lines, like telegraphic wires, dart intelligence to the mind, of any painful impression, and back again through another minute cord, often lying beside it in the same enveloping sheath comes the mandate of the will to meet the exigencies of the case. The finger touches a hot surface, and quicker than thought, the tidings flashes to the brain, which as quickly sends back the mandate for the withdrawal of the suffering member from the destructive contact.

There, too, is the eye, that beautiful window through which the soul looks out upon the surrounding world. Shielded in its bony socket, and with its hairy lash-fringe it has little to fear from either the blow of violence, or the invading dust. The careful eyelid keeps its surface well moistened. Beautifully adjusted muscles roll it in any direction desired. The opening in front admits and measures the needed amount of light, which, passing through its various compartments, paints on the little, acutely sensitive retina, the elements of a landscape many miles in extent, and transmits the needful impression to the brain.

And this delicate little organ, which a ray too much of light offends, which a sand-grain tortures, which a pin-scratch destroys, how rarely is it injured!

As the eye catches the light, the ear takes in sound, which startles the spiritual indweller with the cry of alarm, soothes it with melodies and harmonies, or instructs it with words of wisdom.

As the complicated machinery of the factory is set in motion by the rush of water or the pressure of steam, so the auricular machinery of the human head is set in operation by atmospheric undulations, and one thing moves, and another trembles, and another shakes, and the brain feels, and the mind catches the child's cry, the mother's call, the eloquence of Cicero, or the tramp of battle!

The outside ear gathers in the undulations of the air, and passes them along a little canal, defended with its wax-coating and abattis of hairs against harmful intruders, till they reach a little drumhead stretched across the opening, and fastened at its edges in a strong bony rim. The drumhead, trembling under the touch, shakes a little bone behind it. This bone, like a hammer, knocks upon another of anvil-shape. A point of this anvil disturbs a little bony triangle, and this the liquid in a little chamber behind it. The trembling of this liquid sets up a series of vibrations in a nerve, and the mind hears!

The most moving sounds that enter through the ear are those which come from the human voice. The air passes into and out of the lungs through a chamber curiously wrought with plates, and cords, and valves, variations in the position of which change the breathing into sound; it may be the warblings of a Jenny Lind; it may be a cry of pain. By the aid of the lip, tongue, and teeth, this sound is divided up into articulate speech, into that mystery, the spoken word.

What is such a word? Is it a material or spiritual thing, or neither? It is a thought on wings, a thought riding upon the air, a thought embodied in a sound. But whatever it is, or is not, it is sometimes a thing of immense power. A careless word from the lips of a king once brought the powers of England and France together in a bloody war. A few words from the lips of the present Emperor of the French, made the finances of Europe tremble, and filled her sky with menacing clouds. A British captain, commanding a man-of-war, when he saw some of his men flinch under the broadside of the foe, with fearful imprecations, wished them all in perdition! After the battle, a Christian sailor said respectfully:

"Captain, had your wish been fulfilled, where should we all be now?"

The word went to the captain's heart, and he became a successful preacher of the gospel.

"The ships," writes James in his epistle, "are turned about with a very small helm, so the tongue is a little member, and boasteth great things. The tongue is a fire, a world of iniquity, it defileth the whole body and setteth on fire the course of nature."

And what shall we say of the human hand? In it, as has been well said, we have "the consummation of all perfection as an instrument." In its structure, twenty-nine bones are so adjusted to one another with muscles and delicately formed hinges, as to allow a marvellous facility and variety of action. The fingers when extended are all of different length; but when closed upon the palm, their extremities lie all in the same line. Among its distinguishing features is the long, strong, and variously moving thumb. No small degree of the value of the hand depends upon the facility with which its tip may be brought into contact with the tips of each of the fingers at will. The muscles that play in its motions are chiefly located at a distance so as not to interfere with its raised actions, and the surface is padded so as to keep its mechanism from injury under the strong grasp of the sailor when he hangs his whole weight upon them, of the woodman when he swings his axe, or of the mechanic as he lifts the timber or the heavy stone.

But its strength is even surpassed in interest by the delicacy and velocity of its movements. How the fingers fly over the piano keys!

Now, it is the possession of such an instrument, by such a creature as man, that places him in so high lordship over the physical creation. If he cannot, like Samson, tear open the jaws of a lion, or disengage himself when once in the grasp of the tiger, he can frame an instrument that shall send a leaden ball to meet the monster, and slay him hundreds of feet away. By agency of the hand, matter, vegetable and mineral, soft or hard, is made to take on the forms decreed for it by mind; the forest-tree is transmuted into beautifully wrought and polished furniture; marble, from the quarry, takes on the form of man; the canvass comes to palpitate with the scenes of human life, and the mountain ores are moulded into swords, or pruning-hooks, or into glittering coin. And it is through the fingers that human thoughts pass to the custody of the deathless page.

The feet also are among the marvels of the bodily frame.

"There is no part of the human body more wonderfully constructed than the human feet. They have the requisite strength to support the weight of the human body, and often an additional burden; flexibility, that they may be adapted to the inequalities of the surface on which we tread, and elasticity to assist in walking, running, and springing from the ground. This advantage we possess from the number of the joints, the arch of the foot being composed of twenty-six bones. The bones have considerable play upon each other, and as each articulating surface is covered with cartilage, the essential property of which is elasticity, jarring is thus prevented."

Thus, *standing* is made possible. A problem of great complexity is solved, when a mass of the size of the human body is enabled to stand firmly on so small a basis. A marble statue in human form can be pushed over by a child. *How* it is that man stands so firmly, and with such ease, by what play of the complex machinery of muscles and bones, is a mystery not yet explained; but the effect seems to be due to "a faculty of perpetually shifting the centre of gravity, by a set of obscure, indeed, but of quick-balancing actions, so as to keep the line of direction within its prescribed limits."

There is still another wonder in the human frame that has justly excited admiration. Many of its activities are at the option of the will. Man walks when he will, and talks, or is silent at his own volition; but happily for him his organism is so adjusted as to make many of the most important of these movements independent of his will.

Sir Charles Bell, in his admirable book on the "Human Hand," writes—

"If the vital actions of a man's frame were directed by his will, they are necessarily so minute and complicated, that they would immediately fall into confusion. He cannot draw a breath without the exercise of sensibilities, as well ordered as those of the eye and the ear. A tracery of nervous cords unites many organs in sympathy, of which, if one filament were broken, pain and spasm and suffocation would ensue. The action of his heart and the circulation of his blood, and all the vital functions are governed through means, and by laws, which are not dependent on his will, and to which the powers of his mind are altogether inadequate. For had they been under the influence of his will, a doubt, a moment's pause of irresolution, a forgetfulness of a single action at its appointed time would have terminated his existence."

An act of breathing brings into play a hundred muscles, but man breathes as well when asleep as when awake; and if he would, he cannot voluntarily cease to breathe.

The adjustment of the human frame to the planet on which he lives is another marvel. The power of gravitation draws with a certain force upon the bodily frame, a force too great for the frame enfeebled by disease to resist. Had our planet been twice its actual size, this power would have dragged the strongest man to the surface of the earth.

Thus, too, the jaded light-ray coming with its inconceivable velocity from stars so distant, that thousands of years are spent in the voyage, on reaching our planet, finds the eye of man constructed to take it in and employ it for the purposes of vision. Thus, the strength of the human muscles and bones is nicely adjusted to the size of the orb on which we dwell, and the little eye-ball fitted to the general economy of the universe.

Such is a brief glance at the human body with its vast assemblage of organs working on, day and night, in tireless activity, and playing into each other's hands, the very perfection of harmonious adjustment.

And this china rose which a pebble might dash to pieces, this harp of a thousand strings that dies if one be gone, continues on through countless changes of climate, weather, and temperature, for so many years unbroken and unmarred! In the arid desert, and amid Siberian snows, where his dog will lie down and die from the fierce frigid or torrid extremes, man travels on with impunity. Surely we are wonderfully made!

Had not the Apostle abundant ground for his stirring exhortation,

"I beseech you, brethren, by the mercies of God, that ye present your *bodies* a living sacrifice, holy, acceptable to God, which is your reasonable service."

VIII.

THE WONDERFUL—THE SOUL.

"For though the Giant Ages heave the hill,
And break the shore and evermore
Make and break, and work their will;
Though worlds on worlds, in myriad myriads roll,
Round us each with different powers,
And other forms of life than ours,
What know we greater than THE SOUL!"

IN turning from the body to the soul, we expect to find a wonderful resident in so wonderful a tenement. In kings' houses we look to find those who wear soft clothing. Palaces are not built for paupers, not even by man. When then we find the All-wise constructing an edifice of such elaborate workmanship, to last but a few years, we may be sure that it is for a tenant that God delighteth to honour.

It is true that some have affected to doubt the existence of an immaterial indweller in the physical frame. Reason and science have been suborned to testify that man is twin brother to the soulless brute. Nor is there a more humiliating fact in the history of human thought than that presented in the perverse efforts of the creature made a little lower than the angels to reduce himself to the condition of a full-grown monkey.

"For some philosophers of late, here,
Write, men have four legs by nature;
And that 'tis custom makes them go
Erroneously upon but two."

It has been sharply said, that the only evidence of an origin and nature so mean, is the fact, that some men have been found to believe it. If, indeed, Lord Monboddo, or any one of his followers will claim for himself the dignity of a descent from some ancient and respectable ape, we may not quarrel with the claim, so far as he himself is concerned; but he must not drag the human race down to that level of degradation.

If man knows anything, he knows in his own self-consciousness, that he has an immaterial soul. And, if his consciousness deceives him here, it loses all claim to credence in any of its dictates.

"This frame compacted with transcendent skill
Of moving joints obedient to my will,
Nursed from the fruitful globe like yonder tree,
Waxes and wastes—I call it *mine*, not *me*.
New matter still the mouldering mass sustains;
The mansion changed, the tenant still remains;
And from the fleeting stream repaired by food,
Distinct, as is the swimmer from the flood."

The mind or soul is the self. "I turn my attention on my being, and find that I have organs, and that I have thoughts; my body is the complement of my organs. Am I then my body, or any part of my body? This cannot be. The matter of my body is in a perpetual process of renewal. *I* do not pass away. *I* am not renewed."

"Neither am I identical with my thoughts. They are manifold. I one and the same. Each moment I am aware of the existence or change of my thoughts; this change is sometimes produced by me, sometimes by something different from me; but I always can distinguish myself from them."

It was in the bestowal of a mind, that the Creator stamped his own image upon our nature. A beautiful proof of this resemblance to God is seen in the concord existing between our thoughts and those of God. Cicero has said, in effect, perhaps in "The Tusculan Questions," "that he who can appreciate and approve of the works of God, therein shows that his nature is like that of God." Thus, he who can peruse and comprehend "Paradise Lost," demonstrates that he is a Milton, though perhaps, in many respects, of a far humbler grade. It does not indeed follow, that a mirror that can perfectly reflect a picture, is of the same nature as the painter of the picture. But when this mirror is self-conscious, and taking in all the elements of a painting; sees in it all the painter saw, and appreciates it as thoroughly, he evinces therein the possession of a nature like that of the artist. The ox can see a picture, but cannot appreciate it.

So, when man looks at a flower, comprehending

its parts, approves the plan of its structure, and says to himself: "Had I the power to make such a flower, and wished to reach the ends manifestly aimed at in its formation, I would have adopted just those means of attaining those results," he shows in his perceptions and judgments, that his mind acts just as does the mind that made that flower.

The mind, at birth, may be likened to a watch that has "run down." It is quiescent, and yet with an array of powers that only need the turn of the winding key to set all in motion.

It now begins to perceive, that is, to go out of its material enclosure, and learn of the existence and character of the outer world. Gradually it lays in large stores of knowledge. The bee, too, is a little watch, with embosomed powers, that at maturity, sends it forth upon a certain round of works. What it does, it does well; but we cannot suppose it to know what it is doing, and all its life, it can do no more than it does the first day or week. But man advances in knowledge and skill, and from the wigwam he comes to construct a Coliseum or Cathedral; from the clumsy toy he comes to make a telescope, a steamship, a printing-press.

The bee is perfectly satisfied with the simple monotonous round of activities assigned it in the economy of nature. It asks not how the ants live, nor what the stars are. But man is not, and cannot be satisfied with merely knowing that certain things are. He is impelled, by a resistless inquisitiveness of spirit, to penetrate and comprehend the causes and modes of their existence. If we show a little child, that by burning a bit of paper in a tumbler, and then suddenly inverting the tumbler and plunging it in that position into a basin of water, the liquid will rise and partially fill the glass, he will instantly ask, "Oh, what makes it?"

Man finds out that the planets move in elliptical orbits, that certain mysterious forces impel them in their courses. Cost what it may, he will penetrate to the heart of burning Africa, and to the Arctic pole. There is always within him a "greedy grasping at the distant," and the hidden. He studies plants and animals, learns their habits, and classifies them into orders and families. Armed with certain connate principles or powers of analysis, arrangement, combination and generalization, he produces the whole cyclopædia of the sciences.

He possesses also a strange power of self-modification, and, as it were, of reconstruction. He is crowned by nature with a potent lordship over himself. The tiger must remain ferocious, and the lamb can never make itself other than unresistingly tame and gentle. Man, too, is evidently born with tendencies to certain courses of action, with a certain disposition imbedded in his nature. But it does not follow, that his life will prove a mere development and cultivation of these connate inclinations. If he find himself the subject of strong animal passions, he is not thereby necessitated to become a mere human brute. There may dwell within him a native tendency to miserly penuriousness; and in spite of this he may rise to the dignity of large-hearted liberality. Though, by nature irascible and petulant, he may become meek and kind and forbearing.

He soon becomes aware of a principle within him that approves or disapproves of certain courses of action with himself and others, a principle that impels him to these and dissuades from those, a power that commends or condemns him in what he thinks or does. Certain actions are followed by a glow of pleasure, as if the wings of a bright angel were waving over him, or by a horror of soul, as if dark demons were mocking at and tormenting him.

Scenes equivalent to that fearful one the poet has pictured in Dunsinane have often been realized in human experience—when in the middle of the night Lady Macbeth walks the room, wringing her hands, as if washing them, and exclaiming:

"Yet, here's a spot! Out, I say! One, two! Why, then, 'tis time to do it! Fye, my lord! a soldier, and afraid! Yet, who would have thought the old man had so much blood in him?

"Here's the smell of blood still! All the perfumes of Arabia will not sweeten this little hand! Oh! oh! oh!"

But one of the most impressive facts of the mind, is the memory.

At a very early period, the mind becomes and continues to be a reservoir of ideas, of impressions. Countless items of experience pass into and remain in its recesses. It is highly probable that the mind never parts with an item of knowledge. Thoughts, perceptions, imaginations, volitions, emotions, all those unnumbered items that make up the active life of the soul, enter and remain in the soul a year, five years, for ever! Some of these contents may be summoned back into the consciousness by the mandate of the will, more of them rise to view through the principle of association, but multitudes disappear and may not be recalled for a lifetime. Yet they are there!

Much light is thrown upon the subject by such facts, as the familiar one of the patient in Paris, who, in a fever-delirium, poured forth a torrent of articulate utterances from his lips, utterly unintelligible to his attendants. At length, a person entered who at once perceived that the patient was speaking a patois of one of the remoter provinces of the realm. When the fever passed off, the sufferer could neither speak nor understand the language he so fluently uttered in his ravings, showing that in the depths of the soul one may carry about with him for years the knowledge of a whole language, a knowledge beyond the reach of all his present powers to recall!

Thus, it would seem, man is for ever photographing himself upon himself. He thinks, he feels, he loves, he hates, he speaks, he acts, he weeps, he is merry, and all these acts and experiences engrave themselves in everlasting record upon his deathless soul.

Indeed we are wonderfully made!

IX.

THE WONDERFUL—THE BODY AND SOUL.

"How poor, how rich, how abject, how august,
How complicate, how wonderful is man!
From different natures marvellously mixt!"

WE have, by no means, fathomed the depths of the wonderful in man, till we have encountered the marvels involved in the union between the body and the mind.

The fact of such a union in so circumscribed a system is full of interest. In the great universe, the "macrocosm," we are not surprised at the co-existence of mind and matter, for the line of demarcation is so badly drawn—God, the great spirit yonder on his throne, and matter his footstool and slave. But in this "microcosm," this little universe, they are commingled in a mystery of relationships whose depths no human sounding-line has ever fathomed!

In the characteristics in which these elements, matter and spirit, severally reveal themselves, they are to each other as perfect opposites. Heat and cold, sound and silence, fire and water, light and darkness, life and death, are not more unlike, and mutually opposed. And it is an amazing triumph of divine power and skill, that in human nature they are made to embrace each other and work in harmonious action for the glory of the Creator.

That "prince of philosophers," Sir Wm. Hamilton, quoting words ascribed to Pascal, says, "Man is to himself the mightiest prodigy of nature. For he is unable to conceive what body is, still less what is mind; and least of all, how there *can* be a body and a mind. This is the climax of his difficulties; yet this is his peculiar nature."

But without this union, man is not man. Should a human body be created without a soul, it would not be a man. Were a soul created without a body, this were not a man. Thus, a material body is to the human soul a necessary point of departure from non-existence into being. Once set forth a living self-conscious thing, it plumes its wings for a flight more daring and prolonged than the eagle's; but it cannot begin to fly without a resting-place in a material body at the outset. An essential condition of its existence at all as a human soul, is a converse for a longer or shorter period with flesh and blood, and bones!

A second consideration of intense interest is the *eternity* of this marriage relation between matter and spirit in man. At death there is a temporary divorce of body and soul, but the resurrection re-unites them in a union never to be dissolved.

The mysteries of the separate condition of the

body while bereft of the soul, the dissolution and dispersion of its particles, the distance they travel, the various alliances they form with other organisms, animate and inanimate, their careful preservation, and their instant restoration at the sound of the resurrection trump and reconstruction upon a new and more glorious model, and the re-marriage of body and soul to dwell together for ever, are points upon which devout meditation may well expend its time and strength. It would seem as if the soul had set its inviolable seal upon a given portion of matter that once palpitated with its life, and made them for ever its own.

Upon such points as these we are not careful to answer the suggestions of philosophy. In many things we humbly look up to it, but in matters of revelation such as these, we look far down upon it. Its coffers contain only the guesses of human reason, ours divine revealings. Our faith, so far as believers are concerned, is expressed in these well-weighed and time-honoured words: "The souls of believers are, at their death, made perfect in holiness, and do immediately pass into glory; and their bodies, being still united to Christ, do rest in their graves till the resurrection." At the resurrection, "in a moment, in the twinkling of an eye, the dead shall be raised," "the corruptible" having "put on incorruption," the "mortal," "immortality."

But the marvel, which has most severely taxed the powers of thinking minds ever since philosophy lighted her lamp in a dim antiquity, is the manifest communion of soul and body in the various phenomena of mental and physical life. The view taken of this matter has given a distinctive character to the various philosophies which have, for ages, exercised the acumen of the profoundest minds.

Consciousness, our court of final appeal in such matters, our "intellectual bible," makes no more imperative demand upon our faith than that in perception, volition, and action, the mind and body somehow come together; that there is a reciprocal action and re-action of the one upon the other, that in perception, matter is at once the occasion and object of consciousness; that in volition, determining bodily action, mind actually moves matter.

Yet, here lies the difficulty. How can substances so heterogeneous as the material and immaterial, the extended and unextended, the corporeal and incorporeal come into contact, so to speak, at least into such co-operation as is reported to us in consciousness?

Upon the assumed impossibility of such communion, the materialistic atheist plants himself, and there affects to defy the armies of the living God.

Upon the same ground, Plato denied that God could either create or directly control the material world. Hence, he interposed a "soul of the world," a substance intermediate between God and matter and a kind of mediator between them.

The same difficulty, forbidding any immediate

knowledge of matter, or efficient contact between them, has given birth to all the curious theories which interpose between the perceiving mind and the perceived external world, some substitutionary object, material or immaterial, "images more or less shadowy coming from the object to the mind, or formed by the mind itself, and of itself, in correspondence with the external, real object."

To elucidate this mystery, Des Cartes invented or adopted, and Malebranche developed the noted theory of "occasional causes," which holds, that when the material object is presented, God himself works the result that we call perception. When the mind wills to lift the arm, God, and not the mind, works the muscular result.

Leibnitz would solve the mystery by the theory, that the mental and material worlds are like two separate clocks; the one furnished with the time-keeping, and the other with the striking apparatus; and that such is the harmony divinely pre-established between them, that when the hands of the one point to the given number, the bell of the other strikes off the hour! When the will would move the foot, the foot, of necessity, utterly disconnected with the mind, moves as desired, in virtue of this harmony pre-established between them!

Thus, in the mysteries of this adjustment of mind to matter, and matter to mind, in the human system, God has baffled the skill of the shrewdest, keenest, mightiest minds he ever made! Plato, Des Cartes,

Malebranche, Leibnitz, what names in the catalogue of human thinkers out-mark these? And yet, so wonderful is this mystery, that they stand gazing at it almost like rude savages at an eclipse! The "soul of the world," "occasional causes," "pre-established harmony," splendid fictions of splendid minds, all leave the mystery still as dark and profound as they find it!

Indeed, we are wonderfully made!

X.

THE FEARFUL—MORTALITY.

"Sure 'tis a serious thing to die, my soul!
What a strange moment must it be, when near
Thy journey's end, thou hast the gulf in view!
That mortal gulf by mortal ne'er repassed,
To tell what's doing on the other side!
Nature runs back and shudders at the sight,
And every life-string bleeds at thought of parting!"

We are "fearfully," as well as "wonderfully" made. As already intimated, some of the elements of our nature specified above, are, or may be as full of the formidable as they are of the admirable. Among these is the memory.

"The memory of the eternal *yesterday*
Which ever waning, ever still returns."

This rolling up to the surface of the consciousness of the contents stored up in the mind, is destined to become in many an everlasting torment.

There is profound suggestiveness in the incident recorded of the great philosopher, who, when accosted in the streets by some professor of mnemotechny, with the offer for a certain sum to instruct him in his art, replied:

"I will give you twice that sum to teach me to forget!"

> "Were it not better to forget
> Than but remember and regret?"

Yes, the impossibility of forgetting, the imperative necessity of remembering, will prove to many a terrible endowment.

But the most obvious terror in the constitution of our nature, is our mortality.

"Death, death," iterated and re-iterated a dying apostate, "is a bitter herb!"

The marriage tie between the soul and body is for eternity, and so intimate is their union, and such the nature of their inter-dependence, that the hour of their divorce for a time, is a brief, but real reign of terror—of the king of terrors.

There is the pain of separation, the depth and acuteness of which, whatever may be the speculations and inferences of physicians, or the experience of those who sometimes sink to the gates of death and revive, none but those who have *actually* died can know.

Then, there is the mystery of it. Man may go with secure confidence about his own house in midnight darkness; but set him down in such darkness in a house of which he knows nothing, and his movements will be extremely cautious. Man shrinks from a plunge into darkness.

But death passes man into a state to him utterly unknown. Even the body seems to shrink back appalled from the process and state of dissolution which is to it so like annihilation. And the soul, that as yet has known nothing of unembodied existence, that at the very birth of self-consciousness, found a material arm to lean upon, and ever since, material organs through which to express its life and exercise its powers, shudders to set out alone upon that untried way.

And that human being, body and soul, that at birth found itself in a mother's arms, that during childhood and youth never lacked a brother, sister, or playmate, to share its joys or sorrows, that in maturer life could always, with one loud call, summon kind hearts and hands to its aid, must now leave them all, say farewell to earth and sky, and friends and home, and go forth all alone upon a path he never trod, into a world to him entirely new, and without the possibility of return!

And withal, there are the dread solemnities that overhang this closing up of an earthly career, this sealing up of all earthly accounts with the self and the Creator!

Thus, an inexorable law demands that we shall die, and we are so made that we can die, and therefore, we are "fearfully" made.

XI.

THE FEARFUL—IMMORTALITY.

> "O, listen, man!
> A voice within us speaks that startling word
> Man, thou shalt never die!"

WHATEVER may be said or thought of our mortality, as a fearful element in our nature, it is as nothing to our immortality! That attribute, that constitutes man an imperishable being, is not more wonderful than it is fearful.

True, it has long been the proud claim of man that, in this respect, he ranks high above the soulless brutes that perish.

Poets ring their harmonious changes upon this theme, and think, without all misgiving, that they are crowning man with a chaplet of felicity.

> "Celestial voices
> Hymn it to our souls; according harps,
> By angel fingers touched, when the mild stars
> Of morning sang together, sound forth still
> The song of our great immortality."

Of nothing did Socrates more ardently long to be assured than man's immortality. Of this, Plato strove long and hard to construct a rational demonstration. The noble Cicero would have given his right eye for the removal of all doubt upon this point, and in his discussions he puts this sublime paradox into the mouth of one of his characters:

"I had rather be wrong with Plato in affirming, than right with Democritus in denying this doctrine!"

But with all this, is it not, in a merely rational point of view, a fearful attribute—this of immortality? To be compelled to live for ever; to be doomed to immortality, death, cessation of existence, an everlasting impossibility!

That man is immortal none can rationally doubt, and revelation makes absolutely certain.

In all ages and nations, the soul, of its own instincts, looks to conscious existence beyond the grave, and all theologies have busied themselves with schemes of a future life. The poet has clothed these anticipations in his own fine phraseology:

> "It must be so, Plato, thou reasonest well,
> Else why this pleasing hope, this fond desire,
> This longing after immortality."

> "The soul secure in its own existence, smiles
> At the drawn dagger and defies its point."

It is certainly, at least powerfully suggestive of this truth, that the mind cannot conceive of its own annihilation without a manifest self-contradiction. Every conception of the mind is of necessity accompanied with the conception also of the existence of the conceiving subject. In the conception of a star, there is contained, with the idea, or image of the star, the consciousness of the existence and activity of the conceiving mind. Each conception of the self, contains a double self, the self as the object conceived, and the self as the conceiving subject. Now, with the effort to conceive of the self as annihilated, as non-existent, there of necessity clings to the mind all the way through, the conception of the self, as yet existing and acting, that is of the continued existence of the object it essays to conceive of as non-existent!

One may entertain the proposition—"I shall become non-existent, I may be annihilated." But in the result of the effort to conceive of one's own non-existence, he finds, from the necessity of the case, himself yet existing and conceiving! In other words, the very constitution of our nature makes a conception even of one's own non-existence a palpable self-contradiction and absurdity.

We do not say that this demonstrates our immortality; for the principle applies to the past as well as to the future; but we cannot but think that there is profound significance in the fact, that when once launched into rational existence, we have glided beyond the possibility of a rational conception of our own non-existence.

But this question is for ever set at rest in the word of God. All its great doctrines assume man's immortality, and its chief exhortations charge him to prepare for it.

Come then, what may, as the ages roll on, whatever s rms may beat, conflagrations consume, catastrophes precipitate terrestrial or celestial things to ruin, to you and me, though jaded and foot-sore, distressed or tormented, cessation of conscious existence is an impossibility!

Were there some Lethe whither the soul might hasten in the hour of woe, and bathe itself into eternal unconsciousness, could we but conceal in the folds of the soul's robe some annihilating dagger, or poison, wherewith to end existence in the hour of need, we might with more courage face the future. But this may not be!

I am immortal! I cannot help being immortal! Thou bright sun, when thou hast dismissed thy last ray, I shall live to see thy ashes gathered to their urn and placed away in the recesses of eternal darkness!

Ye stars, though an existence of millions of millions of years be allotted to you, ere I have passed the infancy of my existence, I shall see you fall and die!

And "the hills rock-ribbed and ancient as the sun;" the earth, with all its temples, palaces, and towers, while yet in the dewy morning of my early youth, I shall see them all depart, and like the baseless fabric of a vision, leave not a wreck behind.

Until then, from some source or other, man can obtain assurance that the future state is to be, if not painless, at least, tolerable; until some clear and reliable information can be obtained as to the condition of man during that endless future, it were wiser that he seek to avoid rather than court it.

It is, indeed, often said, that nothing is so dreadful to the mind as the prospect or possibility of annihilation. And no little use is made of this assumption by certain errorists, who teach with a zeal worthy of a good cause the doctrine that the wicked are annihilated at death.

But what is the truth? Many times have we heard the wish uttered with bitter emphasis, "I would to God I had never been born!" From the lips of even the young and the gay, we have heard the wish for annihilation.

And who is not familiar with the passionate, terrible exclamations of the man of Uz in the day of his darkness and woe?

"Let the day perish wherein I was born, and the night in which it was said, here is a man child conceived. Let darkness and the shadow of death stain it; let a cloud dwell upon it; let the blackness of the day terrify it. As for that night, let darkness seize upon it; let the stars of the twilight thereof be dark; neither let it see the dawning of the day: because it shut not up the doors of my mother's womb, nor hid sorrow from mine eyes."

And he that would not prefer annihilation to endless pain and remorse, is a madman! Who would not choose a dreamless sleep before a waking agony?

And, unless we are greatly mistaken, it is vastly

more rational to prefer non-existence to the inexorable necessity of being dragged through an eternity in which anything is possible and everything uncertain.

> "To die—to sleep—
> No more; and by a sleep to say we end
> The heartache, and the thousand natural shocks
> That flesh is heir to—'tis a consummation
> Devoutly to be wished! To die—to sleep—
> To sleep! Perchance to dream! Aye, there's the rub!
> For, in that sleep of death what dreams may come,
> When we have shuffled off this mortal coil
> Must give us pause."

XII.

THE FEARFUL—PAIN.

ALL that is fearful in our nature is tremendously enhanced by our susceptibility to pain.

Among the "Jacula Prudentium" of old father Herbert, is this: "We cry when we are born, and every succeeding day shows why."

For we hourly grow in our capacity to suffer. Man is born a sensitive plant that increases in sensitiveness while life remains. The man can suffer more in an hour than the infant in a week. And when the end comes, we often see man tossed on the billows of a sea of agony, and on these billows he glides from our view. Aside from revelation, it looks as if the future might be a mere continuance of this life, that is, an everlasting growth of our susceptibility to suffer, coupled with, at the very least, a liability every now and then to quiver with anguish in every nerve.

Whether we look at the body, or the mind, we cannot hide it from ourselves, that every faculty and every organ may become an avenue of pain.

The nerves of sensation, if now they are soothed by the balmy breath of spring, may shrink before the freezing blast of winter. The eye, if now it luxuriates in the beauties of the charming landscape, and gazes with delight upon the faces that we love, may also be called to look upon those same faces distorted with agony, or pale in death. Into the ear music may roll her rich and melting harmonies, and the same ear may be compelled to hear the lamentations of sorrow and the wailings of woe.

But what are all possible bodily distresses to those of which the mind is capable? "A wounded spirit who can bear?"

There are woes that course through the soul like streams of burning lava! There are frames of mind to which the brightness of a May morning is odious—the singing of birds grating torture, the merry laugh like the chattering of fiends!

In the afternoon of the 15th of January, 1853, six houses, in process of erection in New York city, suddenly fell, burying several men beneath their ruins. Great was the excitement in that city for a time, but it soon gave way to the din of business, and passed from the general mind. But one day, while surviving workmen were busy restoring the wreck, a female figure, in black, was seen hovering, like a phantom, about the spot. Her eyes were wild, and her manners strange and startling. "Who is that?" whispered one workman to another. "That woman," the other answered, "is the widow of one of the men killed here the other day, and she is a maniac!"

Now, tell us you who have balances in which to weigh human agony, how dreadful and many were the convulsive throes, which shook down the walls of that mind, and buried that woman's reason in ruins heavier far than those that crushed the life out of her husband's frame!

What a thrill went through our land years ago at the tidings wafted to our ears, from across the sea, of that widow's son, now a "thin, loose-jointed boy," exhuming the rocks from the quarry, now enlightening the world upon the fossiliferous treasures of the "old red sandstone," and now gathering the "testimony of the rocks" upon the truth, that all knowledge is a grand duet, revelation playing the celestial, and nature the terrestrial part; and now, his manly frame quivering in agony, till in delirium from an overwrought brain, with his own hand quenching the light of his own life!

Oh, we are fearfully made!

And what a glare of illustration do religious doctrine and religious experience fling upon our capacity to suffer! For, if man, as a religious being, is capable of infinite happiness, as such, he is also capable of infinite misery.

Can any one tell how much distress has been endured by men in view of their condition as sinners yet under condemnation?

The celebrated Dr. John Owen, we are told, when arrested by the Spirit of God, in the midst of his academic honours, with talents that made him the pride of his university, "was so broken down, that for three months he could hardly speak a word to any one, and for five years the anguish of his mind embittered his life."

In the journal of the Rev. David Brainard, we read such records as this:

"One night, I remember in particular, I had opened to me such a view of my sin, that I feared the ground would cleave asunder under my feet and become my grave, and send my soul quick into hell before I could get home. I scarcely dared to sleep, for I thought it would be a wonder if I should be out of hell in the morning."

Some years ago, entering a house, I met a lady just going out on an errand of social enjoyment. After a brief conversation about her soul, I left her, and in her hands a "Baxter's Call."

The next evening, perhaps it was, a ring at my door-bell brought me a message from that lady, begging me to visit her. On entering her room, I found her reclining upon a sofa, in such an agony, as I have rarely seen in a human being. She filled the room and the house with her cries of distress. She was sure that her soul was for ever lost. "Oh," she cried, "tell me of Christ. Tell me how I may be saved! Pray for my poor soul!" For days and nights she continued in a frame of mind bordering on despair, and we all feared that the reason would give way under the terrible pressure, and her mind be plunged into ruins!

Sitting once by an aged and godly man, I listened while he recited the story of his conversion to God. He said:

"When a young man, I was exceedingly profane and wicked. I married, however, a young woman of known, and high-toned piety. On the evening of the first day after we entered our little home, as the twilight was gathering, my wife, without saying a word, set out a little stand by my side with a Bible upon it, and then took a seat on the opposite side of the hearth. I, of course, saw at a glance, what this meant. And there was such a look of confident expectation upon her face, that under a kind of fascination I opened the sacred book, read a chapter, and kneeling down offered a prayer. While thus engaged, such a feeling of horror came over me at the thought of what I, a wretched blasphemer, was doing, as no one ever suffered. I said nothing of this to her, but inwardly avowed that this should be the last time I would be caught in such a service!

The night passed in awful mental distress, and the following day brought no alleviation. In the providence of God, the next evening caught me entrapped in precisely the same way! And when I saw my pious young wife sitting before me and calmly waiting, I had not the power to refuse. Yielding once, made it impossible to refuse now. I repeated the service, and an increasing horror darkened my soul. It continued through the night, and so increased on the following day that I resolved on suicide! I knew there was a rope hanging from the limb of an apple tree in the orchard, and as the evening drew on, and the moment for worship approached, I started from our back door for the orchard! As I went, my anguish increased. I lost, to some extent, the command of my reason. I missed the tree and the rope, and found myself running in the woods. I ran until I fell to the earth and rolled on the ground in agony! While I lay there, it seemed to me for a time, that I was in hell! Suddenly, however, no doubt, in answer to the prayers of others, the light broke; I saw my Saviour in all his beauty and forgiving love, and rose from the ground the happiest sinner that was ever saved; and from that hour to this, I have never known a doubt!"

As the old man told this story with his two hands folded over the top of his staff, his tears rained down upon the floor, and I felt that I was near the gate of heaven.

But sometimes a settled despair gathers over the soul in view of its condition as immortal, and yet for ever lost, the Holy Spirit for ever grieved, the harvest for ever past, leaving it to curse the day of birth, and to wish for annihilation!

In such a case, one sees and feels that he is in the "iron cage."

"So, the interpreter had him into a very dark room, where there sat a man in an iron cage. Now, the man to look upon seemed very sad. He sat with his eyes looking down on the ground, and his hands folded together. Then, said Christian to the man,

"What art thou?"

"I am a man of despair, and am shut up in it, as in this iron cage. I cannot get out. Oh, now I cannot! I have crucified the Lord afresh, and done despite unto the Spirit of grace!"

"But canst thou not now repent and turn?"

"God hath denied me repentance. His word gives me no encouragement to believe. Yea, himself hath shut me up in this iron cage. Oh, eternity, eternity! how shall I grapple with the ills I must meet with in eternity?"

That this is no fancy sketch, many ministers of the gospel can testify from their own observation, and the word of God makes certain.

The door may be shut on the soul for ever even in this life. The voice may go forth of a soul, "Let him alone; he is joined to his idols;" a voice heard by the ministering angels, and by all the means of grace.

"For, if we sin wilfully after that we have received the knowledge of the truth, there remaineth no more sacrifice for sin, but a certain fearful looking for of judgment and fiery indignation, that shall devour the adversaries."

For long, this exclusion from the kingdom of heaven may be unknown and unsuspected by the doomed one. In the meantime, the soul may be as merry as the day is long, as happy as if the name were seen written in the Lamb's book of life. But the conviction of the awful truth may flash upon the mind at any moment. It may come in the midst of life. It may not come until the hour of death; but *when* it comes the spectator may see and know what anguish is!

A pastor informed me of the following, that came under his observation: A young man was arrested by the death-summons in the midst of a life of profligacy. As the last hour drew near, he was seized with an awful horror about the future. He would one while pour out oaths and imprecations, then, fixing his eye upon his mother, he would spring from his bed, and throwing his arms around her neck, beg her to save him! But whenever she proposed to send for a clergyman, he would again break out and rave in blasphemies.

Such torments may men experience in view of their sins and the dreaded penalties.

But even yet, the whole story is not told! Beneath all these depths there lie other deeps still opening wide and threatening to devour—dense darkness, to which all this is but the mere penumbra!

There are yet to be considered, the horrors of the "second death," the death that lives for ever!

It is very remarkable, that nearly all the theologies constructed by man contain a future endless punishment. The enlightened heathenisms of antiquity embraced not only an Elysium, but a Tartarus; a dismal prison surrounded by a triple wall of brass, whose entrance was hidden by a cloud three times more gloomy than the darkest night. Around this wall rolled the fiery river Phlegethon. Its gates of adamant even the gods could not open!

Such is the hell invented by men for themselves! And the words of Jesus say, "These shall go away into *everlasting* punishment." It is "the blackness of darkness for ever." There the "worm dieth not, and the fire is not quenched."

If now, men can suffer as they do this side the grave, what beyond?

Surely, we are fearfully made! All made capable of drinking to the dregs all this varied and concentrated bitterness!

How, then, is it that men can live as we see them living? That the birds spend their days so joyously, leaping from branch to branch, singing their songs, is no marvel; for, though they, too, are wonderfully, they are not fearfully made. But amazement may well possess us when we see human beings living as thoughtlessly as they, singing and dancing, filling the air with their sounds of mirth and revelry, uttering the high oath and the terrible blasphemy!

Do they not know that they are human beings; that as such, they are susceptible to every form of anguish that ever comes to man? Within the bosom of every unpardoned soul there slumbers a magazine of anguish which any day a word of God may explode!

Well may every human being often and deeply meditate upon the fearful elements embedded in his nature!

XIII.

MAN AND THE SON OF GOD.

We have been meditating upon the wonders embosomed in the nature of which we find ourselves partakers.

Another, second to none, for depth of interest and wide-reaching consequences, is found in the alliance of which this nature has been proved capable by the event, with the divine nature.

From all eternity, "before the mountains were brought forth," God existed in himself, by himself, himself the whole universe of being, the uncaused cause of all, uncreated, self-existent.

A chief characteristic of this Divine One is his unity. "Hear, O Israel, the Lord our God is one Lord." The marks of this unity are seen in the all-prevailing harmonies of the created universe, certifying it as the offspring of one mind.

But this unity of God is not of such a character as to exclude all diversity. Man also is a unity in variety, a material nature, and a spiritual nature blended in the harmony of a single person. And the boundless affluence of being in the divine nature embosoms a tri-personality. In the formula of baptism the names of the three persons appear, and in the apostolic benediction, we bless in the name of "the Father, and of the Son, and of the Holy Ghost."

Now, among the decrees on the eternal page, was one fore-ordaining a marvellous and everlasting union, between the loftiest nature in the universe, and the lowest of known created intelligences, between the divine nature in the person of the eternal Son of God and human nature.

The execution of this decree was celebrated above eighteen hundred years ago, when the angels hovering over Bethlehem, shook floods of radiance from their wings and filled the air with their congratulatory songs.

Our world is full of wonders, but the incarnation far outrivals them all. In the little acorn in our hand, we hold not only the cradled oak, but the pregnant germ of countless generations of oak-forests! Bound up in that little bundle are powers which, if the proper conditions be furnished, will produce a tree; that tree will, in the course of its life, give birth to myriads of like acorns, each of which repeat the process, and so on, to the end of time. No thoughtful mind but is staggered at the mysteries wrapped up in that one little seed.

But on that little bundle of life wrapped in swaddling clothes in the Bethlehem manger, angels gaze with amazement, and in its presence, man may well stand with unsandalled feet, and with bowed head, exclaim: "Such knowledge is too wonderful for me. It is high, I cannot attain unto it."

In studying this mystery, we are to bear in mind, that in the incarnation, it was a nature, not a person, that was assumed into union with the Son of God. The alliance was formed, not between a divine person and a human person previously existing, else, as Dr. Shedd remarks in his admirable discussion of this subject in his "History of Christian Doctrine," the result would have been a twofold-self, or rather, two several selves, while in truth, Jesus Christ, the God-Man, was but a single personal self, embosoming two natures; one human, one divine.

The union was effected by the voluntary assumption on the part of the eternal Son of God into alliance with himself of a human nature in the earliest stages of its existence, before it had become an individual person. The human nature of Christ never knew aught of existence separate from him. It was interwoven with himself and constituted into a being in connection with him, moulded by his power, shaped by his will, and conformed to the great eternal design.

"Forasmuch as the children are partakers of flesh and blood," a human nature, "he also himself, likewise," already a person, "took part of the same." (Heb. ii. 14.) "He took not on him," took not hold of "the nature of angels; but took on him the seed of Abraham." It was the seed, the nature in its original elements, that he, by his power, blended with his own nature in one divine-human, human-divine personality.

In this procedure, of course, the Son of God acts in pure sovereignty, as he forms a union not with an individual human person with a will of its own, but with an elementary human nature not yet become a person.

The immediate result of this assumption is the person thereby constituted. In this strangely constituted person, there exists two complete unmutilated natures, a perfect human nature, and a perfect divine nature, as in an ordinary human person we find an animal nature blended with a mental nature. In this union, neither nature parts with any attribute properly belonging to it, in itself considered.

"The only Redeemer of God's elect is the Lord Jesus Christ, who being the eternal Son of God became man, by taking to himself a true body and a reasonable soul." "The Word was made flesh." In this new person the basis and all-controlling element is the second person of the blessed trinity.

This predominant nature is not merely like, but actually is God.

Adam was like God. He was made in his image. He was like him in being perfectly holy; like him in his moral perceptions. Two chords of a musical instrument were never attuned to harmony so complete as that with which the moral nature of man originally responded to that of his Creator.

He was like him in dominion over the lower

creation. God divided terrestrial creatures into two classes; the lordly and the subject races. In one he placed man, and beneath him the fish of the sea, and the fowl of the air, and every living thing that moveth upon the earth. All these man might catch and kill, buy and sell, and yoke to his uses.

He was like God in his immortality, and from the moment of his creation, his duration runs parallel with that of God.

Neither is the Redeemer a mere human being, inhabited as it were by a divine power.

Such were the Prophets and Apostles as inspired men. "The Spirit of God spake by me," wrote David, "his word was in my tongue." "Holy men of God spake as they were moved by the Holy Ghost."

The Spirit of God dwells in all believers. "Know ye not that ye are the temple of God, and that the Spirit of God dwelleth in you."

Men of genius are in an important sense the subjects of divine influence.

"And the Lord spake unto Moses, saying: See, I have called by name Bezaleel the son of Uri, and I have filled him with the Spirit of God, in wisdom, and in understanding, and in knowledge, and in all manner of workmanship, to devise cunning works, to work in gold, and in silver, and in brass."

David blesses God, who taught his "hands to war and his fingers to fight."

Hence, the appropriateness of the sublime apostrophe of Milton in the opening of Paradise Lost, assuming that there was in the poet's breast a tone of true devoutness.

> "O, Spirit, that dost prefer
> Before all temples the upright heart and pure,
> Instruct me, for thou knowest.
> What in me is dark,
> Illume! what is low, raise and support;
> That to the height of this great argument
> I may assert eternal providence,
> And justify the ways of God to man."

The higher nature in the Redeemer was purely and properly and perfectly divine, "very God of very God." "The Word was God."

"When he bringeth in the first-begotten into the world, he saith, And let all the angels of God worship him. *Unto* the Son, he saith, Thy throne, O God, is for ever and ever."

"We are in him that is true, even in his Son Jesus Christ. This is the true God and eternal life."

The second and inferior element in the person of the Redeemer, is truly, purely, perfectly human.

His body was a true human body, not a seeming body, a phantom body, assumed temporarily for a purpose, to be put off at death. "Behold!" said Jesus, after the resurrection, "behold my hands and my feet, that it is I myself: handle me and see; for a spirit hath not flesh and blood, as ye see me have."

His tears were true human tears. His blood was true human blood.

But this human nature was more than a mere

body, a mere mass of animated flesh. This alone were no human nature. A mere body, in whatever form, without a soul, is not a human, but a merely animal nature. But Christ took to himself "a true body *and* a reasonable soul," a soul replete with all the attributes and endowments of a complete human spirit. Hence, he was subject to all the common emotions, sympathies and susceptibilities of our nature.

He loved his country, and in the tears that rolled down his cheeks, as he wept over doomed Jerusalem, patriotism had a share. He was a true philanthropist, and his bosom burned with love for his adopted race. Friendship kept her altar-fires kindled in his heart, and he "loved Martha and her sister, and Lazarus," and he "loved his disciples to the end." "Whosoever shall do the will of my Father which is in heaven, the same is my brother, and sister, and mother." Nor were pure domestic affections wanting. He loved his mother, and tender thoughts of her moved within him, even on the cross.

Now, both these natures, the human and divine, were blended in one person. All the experiences of the Messiah were those of this complex, but single person.

Had there been two selves, then, as has been well said, as only the human nature can suffer, Christ's sufferings would have been inadequate to the work of the atonement. The penal sorrows he endured must possess an infinite value, which to those of a merely human self were utterly impossible. As it was, his agonies, though strictly borne in the humbler nature, received a value from its alliance with the higher, such as to render them infinitely precious and effective. As the suffering, not of a merely human self, but of a self divinely human, humanly divine, they avail to pay all human debts, satisfy divine justice, and reconcile us to God.

In this complex person, the divine nature was in constant and commanding control, blending the human with itself, sanctifying and glorifying all its powers and susceptibilities.

We are thus enabled to understand and explain many of those otherwise startling paradoxes of inspiration. For in the sacred writings, whatever may be affirmed of either nature, is affirmed of the person.

As with man, when one says: "I thirst," it is the man, the person that thirsts, although the appetite has its root in the physical nature. And when the poet writes—

> "Oh, for a lodge in some vast wilderness,
> Some boundless contiguity of shade,
> Where rumours of oppression and deceit
> May never reach me more!"

it is the man, the person that longs, though the longing comes up from the depths of a noble moral and intellectual nature.

And when Jesus says, "I and my Father are one," this is true of Jesus, the Messiah of the complex, theanthropic person, but the affirmation is based strictly upon the divine element in that person.

And when he says, "My Father is greater than I," this, also, is true of the person; but this affirmation is grounded strictly upon the lower constituent nature in that person.

"Before Abraham was, I am." "The Son of man who is in heaven," and such like passages, are true of the speaker, and yet refer us directly to the divine element. "They crucified the Lord of glory." "The church which he hath purchased with his own blood." These passages also are true of the person, but point us strictly to that nature in that person which alone is capable of suffering.

"They shall call his name Emmanuel, which being interpreted is, God with us."

Sometimes a banner is put into the soldier's hands inscribed with the name of battles he has fought and won, and how fondly he gazes upon its folds as they rise and fall on the breeze, and what nerve the sight of it imparts when another battle draws on!

But this banner passed from the angels to Jesus' hand, in behalf of the race, betokening the alliance between God and man in our nature. Who can tell the whole power and felicity of its influences upon mankind? Governments have been moulded by it. Legislation has acknowledged its influence, and all literature has experienced its power!

No other regiment in all the host of God can carry such a banner. It waves over the towers of no other city in all the empire of Jehovah!

Now, do we not find in the fact, that our nature is adapted to such a union with the divine, a chief one among the wonders that challenge our admiration? There are many creature-natures with which we cannot conceive such a union to be formed. Had the angelic nature been chosen so far as we are able to understand that nature, such a union would have been far less strange and surprising than the alliance with ours.

And does not this union disclose to us a new and profound significancy in the declaration that man is made in the image of God?

The decrees of God are one eternal purpose. The perfections of the divine nature forbid the conception of any succession in those decrees. His plans are in no sense a construction implying any after-thought and addition. In our mode of conceiving of them, we are constrained by the nature of our minds to recognize a certain logical order in them. But in the divine mind they are all, as it were, one complete picture.

Ruskin, in his "Modern Painters," contrasts the mental processes of an ordinary artist with that of a first-class genius. The one constructs his picture and puts his conceptions together piecemeal. The other conceives a given work at once as a whole. One constructs, the other creates. One conceives, say, the trunk of a tree, then fits on its branches and twigs and foliage, changing and readjusting until the object is shaped to his judgment. The other sees the whole tree at a glance, in all the perfections of its outline and proportions, and thence has nothing to do but to embody the conception in lines and colours on the canvass.

Rising from the finite to the infinite, from man to God, we must conceive of the Divine Being, as having from all eternity before his mind, so to speak, a perfect picture of the predestinated universe in all its completeness. In his book all its members were written, which in continuance, were fashioned when as yet there were none of them. Actual creation has added nothing, can never add anything to this preconceived creation. Every atom of matter, with all the successive forms through which it was destined to pass, from the beginning to the end of time, every sentient creature, with all the events in the history of each, what each should be, do, and suffer, were all there in that original plan.

Hence, we may say, the universe as truly existed for God before, as after the actual forth-putting of creative power. It is not so with the artist. His statue on the pedestal is more a real substantive thing than it was while it lay in ideal in his mind. But with God, the thing decreed is as instinct with reality before, as after its creation. The execution of the purpose embodying the eternal thought gives that object no new substantial being with God.

Now, since the parts of the universe are all adjusted to one another in perfect harmony in the decree, we must assume that the marvellous nature ordained for man, with all that makes it wonderful and fearful, had original reference to the relationship it was to bear to the divine nature in the person of the eternal Son, not only here on earth, but in heaven above. There for ever, the heavenly host are to behold their king, "a Lamb, as it had been slain." The sceptre, at whose uplifting they bow, is in the hand of Him "who liveth and *was dead*, and who is alive for evermore." In the blessed economy of heaven, the Son sits on the throne in the glorified body carried with him thither, at the ascension from Olivet's crest. Thus, the heavenly host see for ever in their king an incarnate God, our nature in eternal alliance with the Deity, "God and man in two distinct natures, and one person for ever."

In the image of this eternal king, in the form which the eternal Son of God was for ever to wear upon the throne he won by his condescension, his birth, life and death, ("wherefore God hath highly exalted him, and given him a name which is above every name: that at the name of Jesus *every* knee should bow, of things *in heaven*, and things in earth, &c.") man was made, and therefore, again he was "wonderfully made."

XIV.

MAN AND THE GOD-MAN.

ANOTHER chapter of wonders awaits our perusal in the mysteries and glories involved in the union subsisting between Christ, the God-man, and each soul on whom his atoning blood has been sprinkled.

First, we find man, in himself, an inexplicable mystery, combining in his person a blending of a material, and a spiritual nature. Then, we find this marvellous nature taken into alliance with the Son of God in the mysteries of the incarnation. The climax of all is reached in an additional union between the ransomed soul and the ransoming Redeemer.

For "we are members of his body, and of his flesh, and of his bones. This is a great mystery, but I speak concerning Christ and the church."

"I am the vine, ye are the branches." "Inasmuch as ye have done it unto one of the least of these my brethren, ye have done it unto *me*."

The *body* participates in this union. "The body is for the Lord." "Know ye not that your bodies are members of Christ."

On this passage (1 Cor. vi. 15,) Dr. Charles Hodge remarks: "Our bodies are the members of Christ, because they belong to him, being included in the redemption effected by his blood, and also, because they are so united to him as to be partakers of his life. It is one of the prominent doctrines of the Bible that the union between Christ and his people includes a community of life, and it is clearly taught that this life pertains to the body as well as to the soul."

Nor does death, which temporarily divorces the soul and body, interrupt or suspend this membership with Christ. And it is this relationship that secures a glorious resurrection. "If the Spirit of him that raised up Jesus from the dead dwell in you, he that raised up Christ from the dead shall also quicken your mortal bodies by his Spirit that dwelleth in you." "Our bodies being still united to Christ, do rest in their graves till the resurrection."

Death is called a sleep, and saints are said to "sleep in Christ;" but this is true only of their bodies. The soul does not fall asleep; for it, "to be absent from the body, is to be present with the Lord." But, if the body participates in this strange union, it is because it is drawn in thither by the soul, and the channel through which the soul glides into this relationship, is faith. The vine clings to the supporting tree by its tendrils; the tendrils of the soul are the forth-puttings of faith.

By nature, the vine, weak and helpless, crawls

along upon the ground. At length, it reaches a tree and begins to climb. One tendril after another clasps a twig here, and a twig there, and at length, the naturally grovelling becomes a towering vine, and swings in the air at the tree's very top. So, by nature, the soul crawls and grovels, and hugs the ground. But when it reaches the Son of God, the tree of life, and puts out its tendrils, it mounts and mounts, and embracing the tree all around, so becomes one with it, that the axe that smites the one, smites the other, and no tornado, not strong enough to uproot the tree, can dislodge the vine from its resting-place.

Thus, faith is the connecting link between the believer and the Redeemer. A stone forms part of an edifice by position. A foreigner becomes one with a nation by naturalization. Man is joined in happy relationship with his neighbour by friendship. By marriage, a more intimate and profound relationship is constituted, and "they twain become one flesh."

Now, between Christ and man, faith is a marriage tie. Christ is the bridegroom. The soul is the bride. The Christian pastor is the friend of both, who, standing by, greatly rejoiceth at the bridegroom's voice. The bridal party is composed partly of the membership of Christ's body, the believing saints, and partly of the angels, who fill heaven with their gratulatory songs when this union is once effected.

The moment the marriage vows are uttered, man and woman are one flesh. The moment man exercises saving faith, he and Christ are one. The act of faith is an act of transfer, by which one leaps the chasm of unbelief and is clasped in the arms of the Saviour, in a grasp never to be relaxed, for ever and ever.

But we must go one step farther back to find the origin of this alliance.

The vine clasps the tree through the agency of its tendrils; but whence come the tendrils? These come from the inresident life of the plant that extrudes them from its own bosom. They issue from the depths of its vitality.

But in man by nature, as a religious being, there is no life. "In Adam, all die." The vine is dead. Hence, it can neither move towards the tree, nor push out tendrils to grasp it.

Whence comes the life? The source of this is the eternal Spirit of God. "Born," brought into life, "not of flesh, nor of the will of the flesh, nor of the will of man, but of God." "Born of the Spirit." It is "by one Spirit that we are baptized into one body." The agent in this work is the Holy Spirit, "convincing us of our sin and misery, enlightening our minds in the knowledge of Christ, and renewing our wills, he doth persuade and enable us to embrace Jesus Christ freely offered to us in the gospel." The tree is Jesus Christ. The gospel plants that tree in human soil within reach of the human soul. Then, the Spirit, by a creative, regenerating act, implants a life which becomes the basis of a new series of activities. Interweaving with itself the native contents of the soul, the understanding, the will, and the affections, it sets them upon a new course of action. New perceptions arise, new thoughts, new motives, new emotions, new purposes. By virtue of these new powers, the vine leaves the ground, and grasps and climbs the tree.

Or, recurring to the marriage scene, it is the Holy Spirit of God that stands as the officiating priest, marrying the soul and the Saviour into a union, whose felicities are as great as its mysteries are profound.

These mysteries are as baffling (but no more so) as those of the union between the material and immaterial in human nature, as those of the human and divine natures in the Messiah, as those of the trinity.

The felicities of this union are of greater magnitude and preciousness than we ever shall know till we have left

> "This bank and shoal of time,"

and found ourselves upon the bank of life's river in the skies.

A common life now pervades the God-man and the redeemed man. As the plant-life takes hold of and interweaves with itself the life of the engrafted twig, so the Christ-life takes hold of and entwines with itself the life in the soul. Whatever befals the one includes the other. When the persecutor smites a saint, he smites Christ. "Saul, Saul, why persecutest thou *me!*" "In all their afflictions he is afflicted." Many are the afflictions of the righteous, but in all of them they are only "filling up that which is behind of the afflictions of Christ."

And they die in Christ. "I am crucified with Christ." They bear the penalties of the law in Christ, and with him. They live in and with Christ. "*Because* I live, ye shall live also." They rise with Christ. His resurrection involves and necessitates theirs. They ascend with him to heaven, and there reign with him for ever and ever.

A beautiful and precious result of this union is seen in the closeness of the bonds thus established among the brotherhood of the faithful.

The question of external union among the various tribes of believing Israel, is ever recurring. All wish for it. All pray for it. The sacred petition of Jesus is ever on their lips. "That they may all be one; as thou, Father, art in me, and I in thee, that they also may be one in us. I in them, and thou in me, that they may be made perfect in one."

Nor are these yearnings a mere freak of vain-dreaming enthusiasm. They grow out of the actual, constitutional union, now subsisting between the great vine and the branches. They are the yearnings of different members of a divided family for the removal of all causes of division, and a complete and visible family union.

For already they are actually "one in Christ." In him "there is neither Jew nor Greek, there is neither bond nor free."

Go out under the unclouded sky of night and look up at the stars. They seem to lie in unarranged confusion, as if the Creator had sown them broad-cast over the heavens, as the farmer sows seed in a field. Each one seems to trim its silver lamp and hold up its burning censer before God in entire isolation from its bright-robed companions. But the truth is, that a cord strong as the will of God, holds every primary in its place, and binds the secondaries to their several centres.

And send the ribald scoffer through the world, and he will doubtless find abundant diversity, not to say disorder among the members of the household of faith. Here, a band of Christians will be found worshipping after one mode, there after another. With this denomination, special, and even inordinate stress is laid upon one doctrine or ordinance, and with that upon another. Nay, at times he will find those who acknowledge each other as Christians in the true sense of the word, arrayed against each other, as foe against foe, here exulting in controversial triumph, there chagrined with a sense of discomfiture. One lives in the luxurious ostentation of a prince, another amidst the privations of extreme poverty, in the bonds of slavery, or even begging upon the king's highway. One fills the professor's chair in the academy, and another, doubting that the earth is round, and that it revolves upon its axes, knows only that he has a soul, is a lost sinner, and that Christ died to save. One wears the black skin of the African, another the red skin of the American Indian, and another the fair skin of the Caucasian.

But, differing and alienated, and even hostile, they are still all one in Christ. "We being many, are one body in Christ, and every one members one of another. For as many of you as have been baptized into Christ, have put on Christ."

And why may we not hope that this vital, constitutional union, expressing itself in these yearnings for a union that is external and visible, shall be one day fully realized? The church is one. The truth is one. And when this one church, freed from dividing imperfections, comes to see this one truth just as it is, what will remain as a ground-work and cause of division?

XV.

MAN AND HEAVEN.

"Who are these in bright array,—
This innumerable throng,—
Round the altar night and day,
Tuning their triumphant song?
Worthy is the Lamb once slain,
Blessing, honour, glory, power,
Wisdom, riches to obtain;
New dominion every hour."

In the marvellous constitution of our nature, fitting it for union with the eternal Son in the incarnation, and with the God man by faith in regeneration, we see a manifest pre-adaptation for the honours and glories assured in the word of God, to all who, washed and made white in the blood of the Lamb, find their way into the mansions of bliss.

Few accessible objects have eluded the prying inquisitiveness of the human mind; but, as yet, no instance has been discovered of a living creature not manifestly so adapted to surrounding circumstances as to fit it for enjoyment.

Even the much-talked-of sloth is found to be no exception to this law. The apparently disproportionate length of its arms, as compared with its legs, being nearly twice their length, the structure of its feet and claws, curved inwards to such a degree as to compel it, when attempting progression on a plane surface, slowly and painfully to drag itself along on its elbows, suggested the idea that it was, as it were, a kind of creative mistake, doomed to a precarious and wretched life. But when it is found to be an arboreal quadruped, born, living, and dying in the trees, whose proper mode of progression is along the branches and twigs, hanging beneath and passing one foot over the other in an easy, and by no means tardy, progress, it becomes another proof and illustration of divine wisdom and goodness.

It is little likely, therefore, that man, the wonderfully-framed monarch of all, should be an exception to this beneficent law. He desires happiness, and was evidently made for enjoyment.

Sin, in making him miserable, plunged him into an abnormal condition. Christ came to cancel sin, and thus removing the cause of all sorrow to restore man to his normal happy condition.

This restoration, however, is not complete in this life. Cares still burden, suspense harrasses, apprehensions vex, disappointment weighs him down, sickness wears him out, and then his spirit is conveyed to another and a better world.

In that better world, all sources of discomfort disappear, and everything around ministers to his bliss. Poetry and inspiration combine to picture the scenes of enjoyment above, and yet confessedly fail, partly through the feebleness of language to express, and the incapacity of finite minds to conceive of the actual condition there, to do more than produce the impression that those joys are boundless.

In the last chapters of Revelation, the original paradise is not only reproduced, but all its glories are infinitely magnified. The first paradise is a garden, and so is the last. But in this last, there is no forbidden tree. Besides this, the felicities of the first are enhanced by the addition of all that is fascinating and improving in social life, and in the richest results of a perfect civilization. The glories of a splendid city are added to those of a perfect garden. Heaven is represented as a garden in a city. The city is spacious,—fifteen hundred miles square. The wall is of jasper, its foundations garnished with all manner of precious stones, and its twelve gates are so many pearls. The streets are paved, and lined with edifices of pure, transparent gold.

The height of the city is also fifteen hundred miles. In this, perhaps, we may find allusion to those great and splendid cities of antiquity with which John was familiar, most of which contained towering eminences crowned with edifices, upon which art had lavished all its gifts and wealth all its treasures. Over the streets of Ephesus, the temple-crowned heights of Prion and Coressus threw their long shadows. Upon Athens, the Acropolis looked down the central base, as the rhetoricians said, of a vast fire-circled shield, the outer four of the circles being the city, Attica, Greece, and the world—the Acropolis itself "one vast composition of architecture and sculpture, dedicated to the national glory and the worship of the Gods."

Corinth had her renowned Acrocorinthus, towering abruptly upward, two thousand feet above the city. Its lofty summit, from which the Acropolis of Athens, forty-five miles away, was distinctly visible, afforded room for a whole town.

The heaven of the man of Patmos had its temple-crowned Acropolis fifteen hundred miles high! On its top was the throne of God, from out of which flowed the "river of water of life, clear as crystal," now gliding through a plain, now leaping in cascades, now lingering on the terraces, and now thundering down in magnificent rapids! On either side was the tree of life, bearing twelve manner of fruits, each yielding its fruit every month.

All this, of course, is only the affluence of oriental imagery, struggling through the holy impulses of inspiration, to tell us that the glories of heaven cannot be told! It conveys permission to the sanctified fancy to plume its wings for its loftiest possible flights in the effort to compass some conception of what awaits the glorified.

But the crowning glory of even this heaven is found in the rank assigned to ransomed mortals in this world of glories. It were enough that man were admitted within the gates of this city-paradise, and we can comprehend the raptures of the saintly Rutherford, when he wrote, "Though I never enter those pearly gates, I shall be content if I may but from outside the walls be permitted to throw my praises over into the lap of my Lord!"

But the saints are not kept outside the walls. They do not even occupy the mansions on the lower terraces of the city. Their home is in the Acropolis! They compose the very court of heaven! The angels are farther from the throne than they!

The "new song" in heaven, that awakens its highest raptures, is one the angels cannot sing, but to which they only respond with their joyous, cordial amen! They can never say "Unto Him that loved us and *washed us* from our sins in his own blood."

The Son of God has never come into such relations with the angels, nor done for them as he has for man. He never lifted a burden from an angel's soul, nor wiped a tear from an angel's cheek. He never saw an angel mother bending over a coffin that contained the remains of a precious babe, nor an angel widow faint on the edge of the grave in which lay the remains of her dearest friend and sworn protector. But all who from earth join the throng around the throne, go up thither out of great tribulation.

"And one of the elders answered, saying unto me, what are these which are arrayed in white robes, and whence came they? And I said unto him, Sir, thou knowest. And he said unto me, These are they which came out of *great tribulation*."

"Once they were mourning here below,
And wet their couch with tears;
They wrestled hard, as we do now,
With sins and doubts and fears."

No angel in heaven is indebted to Christ for the pardon of a sin, and hence, they are not bound to him by the ties of love gushing from hearts grateful for rescue from an awful perdition.

"Jesus said: Simon, I have somewhat to say unto thee. There was a certain creditor which had two debtors: the one owed five hundred pence, and the other fifty. And he frankly forgave them both. Tell me therefore, which of them will love him most?

"Simon answered, and said, I suppose that he to whom he forgave most. And he said unto him, Thou hast rightly judged."

But all who ascend from earth to dwell at God's right hand, have received forgiveness of countless transgressions, and each will sing for ever—

"Love I much, I'm much forgiven,
I'm a miracle of grace."

Of the two sons in the parable, he who loved his father most tenderly was the returned prodigal. And we may be sure that there is no such love for the Son of God in heaven, as that which glows in hearts that have been snatched, as brands plucked out of the burning, from everlasting woe, and gathered to eternal joy through the sprinkling of atoning blood.

But the fountain of all the wealth of felicity, there poured into human coffers, is found in that strange alliance which makes each ransomed one a member "of his body and flesh and bones." No such alliance has been formed with the angels. "He took not on him the nature of angels."

"Not angels round the throne
Of majesty above,
Are half so much obliged as we,
To our Immanuel's love."

"They never sunk so low;
They are *not raised so high;*
They never knew such depths of woe,
Such heights of majesty."

"The Saviour did not join
Their nature to his own;
For them he shed no blood divine,
Nor breathed a single groan."

Hence, even on earth, the angels are the servants of the ransomed. "Are they not all ministering spirits, sent forth to minister for them who shall be heirs of salvation?" They take a profound interest in all that concerns them.

"He bids his angels pitch their tents
Round where his children dwell;
What ills their heavenly care prevents,
No earthly tongue can tell."

They rejoice over their conversion. "There is joy in the presence of the angels over one sinner that repenteth." At death, the angels bear the soul to Abraham's bosom.

And in the rapt visions of John, in Patmos, we always see the saints nearer to, and the angels farther removed from, the throne.

"And I beheld, and lo, in the *midst* of the throne, and of the four living ones, and in the *midst* of the elders, stood a Lamb, as it had been slain."

And when the Lamb "had taken the book, the four living ones, and the four-and-twenty elders fell down *before* the Lamb." Who these elders and living ones represent, we learn in their song.

"Thou art worthy to take the book and to open the seals thereof: for thou wast slain and hast redeemed US to God by thy blood."

And then the angels *round about* the throne, *and* the living ones, *and* the elders, thus redeemed, sing their responsive song.

"Worthy is the Lamb that was slain to receive power, and riches, and wisdom, and strength, and honour, and glory, and blessing."

In accordance with this idea of special nearness of the saints to God in heaven, is the proclamation.

"Behold the tabernacle of God is *with men*, and he will *dwell with them*, and they shall be his people, and God himself shall be with them."

The reason given of this special nearness, is the mark of his purifying blood on their white garments.

They have washed their robes and made them white in the blood of the Lamb. "*Therefore*, are they *before* the throne of God, and serve him day and night in his temple: and he that sitteth on the throne shall dwell among them."

"Know ye not," writes Paul, "that we shall judge angels?" that in the arrangements of the final economy, the angels will hold a position inferior to that of the blood-ransomed, blood-washed saints of the Lamb.

Well may the believer exclaim, in view of such prospects, of all that is involved in the glories and felicities of such a nearness to the throne of heaven, and for the mysteries of such a relationship to its once crucified occupant—"Oh, the depth of the riches, both of the wisdom and knowledge of God! How unsearchable are his judgments and his ways past finding out."

"Such knowledge is too wonderful for me. It is high, I cannot attain unto it!"

XVI.

MAN AND RELIGION.

In the light of the truths now discussed, and, especially in view of the wonderful, fearful nature we bear, the adaptedness of true religion to our condition stands forth in bold relief. It glorifies all that is wonderful, and furnishes also the alchemy by which all that is fearful is transmuted into the brightest jewels in the human casket.

Who can parry, or reply to the charge of the infinite folly of squandering the affluence of such a nature upon the sensual and evanescent, and the sin and shame of sacrificing it on the altar of profligacy, and thus, not only robbing it of all the glories proffered in the mystic alliance with the God-man, and the exaltation and bliss of an eternal heaven, and God of a lamp that else might shine for ever with others around his throne, but, also taking security for everlasting woe!

Cleopatra, at the banquet given to Anthony, at Tarsus, (afterwards the birthplace of Saul,) is said to have dissolved a pearl, worth fifty thousand pounds sterling, in vinegar, and swallowed it at a draught! That pearl "might have been sold for much, and given to the poor."

But, what is even the insane extravagance of that profligate queen, when compared with his, who dissolves, as it were, the pearl of such a nature as ours, in the cup of three-score years and ten, of easy, wild, worldly voluptuousness?

Belshazzar perpetrated an act of fatal folly, when he lighted up a heathen banquet with the golden candlestick, from the Holy Place, in the temple of Jehovah. And what do they, who, at the ordinary feast of secular life, burn out all the fires of a human nature?

We blush, and weep together, when we see, as we so often do, talents, intellectual, and other, that might adorn our literature, might certify and purify legislation, multiply hospitals, asylums, and institutions of learning, making education more efficient and more generally accessible, make two blades of grass to grow in the place now filled by one, build comfortable tenements for the worthy, toiling poor, in a word, do many of the ten thousand things that go to replenish the cup of national prosperity and social happiness, thrown away in unmeaning and unmanly trifling!

But, what is even this, in comparison with the course of him, who, in the endowments of a human nature, possessing the means of glorifying God, of serving heaven for himself, and of leading many others thither, lavishes all upon pursuits and pleasures, which, at length, leave the exhausted spirit to the lamentation of the expiring Talleyrand.

"Behold! eighty-three years passed away! What cares! What agitations! What anxieties! What complications! What ill-will! And all without other result than great fatigue of body and mind, a profound sentiment of discouragement for the future, and of disgust for the past!"

And, if angels ever shudder, they do it at the sight of the man who takes his marvellously, fearfully framed body, with its mysterious, immortal tenant, and lays it a living sacrifice to be burned to ashes on the altar of drunkenness and debauchery!

And, who can measure the catastrophe, and compass its full magnitude, when a nature, such as man's, folds the wing that might have soared to the highest heavens, and sinks like a mill-stone from an angel's hand, into eternal woe! Well might the prophet write—

"Hell, from beneath, is moved to meet thee at thy coming! It stirreth up the dead for thee. All they shall speak and say unto thee—Art thou also become as weak as we? Art thou become like unto us? How art thou fallen, Lucifer, son of the morning!"

And how admirable the adaptation of true religion to meet the exigencies of human nature!

In all that is wonderful in man, we see only the adjustment of a harp of many strings to thrill with the most rapturous harmonies.

The action of the powers of thought upon merely secular objects, is often attended with rich enjoyment. The logician, as he forges link into link, in the chain of close consecutive reasoning; the orator, as he pours his soul-stirring sentences upon the ears of listening multitudes; the artist, as the bright conception flashes upon him, and he burns to transmit it to the canvass, or embody it in marble; the poet, "his eye with fine frenzy rolling," as he enshrines his thoughts in enduring lines; the philosopher, as he pursues the paths of investigation in the world of nature, all find in the excitement of thought itself, an intense enjoyment.

But when the heavenly replaces the earthly, as an object of thought, and the finite mind, now in saving alliance with the infinite, pursues such themes as man's redemption, the legislation of heaven for human salvation, the processes by which a sin-smitten world is washed of its defilements, and its ruins built into a temple for the living God, in a word, any of all the grand themes of revelation, it has reached a terrace, where balmier airs fan the brow, sweeter music greets the ear, and brighter prospects gladden the eyes. And all the play of the moral nature, now in conscious harmony with that of God, brings with it its own peculiar reward.

The memory, too, busied with recollections of gracious providences, and gracious exercises, by and through which the soul passed from death to life, and the various scenes of spiritual enjoyment through which it has been led, becomes a new treasure in its coffers.

The play of the affections, now divorced from the odious and sinful, and throwing their tendrils around that which is pure and enduring, mingles drops, new and sweet, in the cup quaffed by the soul.

And this mind with all its powers, washed of all defilement, relieved of all weaknesses, and instinct with the vigour of the life above, how will it lash with its sanctified and glorified wing, the air of heaven, and sing and soar while eternity lasts?

If we turn from the wonderful to the fearful, in our nature, just as the rising sun floods the clouds in the horizon with hues more in number, than man can name, so does the religion of our Lord gild all these fearful things into felicities!

Take our capacities to suffer. They are no longer fearful. For these capacities simply make suffering possible, not necessary. But, at my Saviour's side above, what afflictive causes can ever reach me?

Even here, how sorrow's cup is robbed of its bitterness! The period during which suffering is possible, is very limited. They are "but for a moment." Who cannot suffer anything for "a moment," when he knows that then the griefs not only come to a perpetual end, but usher the patient into everlasting bliss? Through all our griefs this one commanding truth confronts us, that we are now engaged in bearing all the ills that will come upon us, for ever and ever!

Then, invaluable mitigations, in many forms, mingle sweets in the bitter cup. The Spirit of God dwelling in the soul, nerves up its powers to endure, and the effect is the same, whether the burden be diminished, or the strength increased. And we have ever at hand the "Rock of Ages," into whose clefts we may run, as a "hiding-place from the wind, a covert from the tempest, rivers of water in a dry place, and the shadow of a great rock in a weary land."

Sympathy of the loving in our struggles, makes them easier. "And in all our afflictions, HE is afflicted."

"Fear thou not, for I am with thee. Be not dismayed, for I am thy God. I will strengthen thee, yea, I will help thee; yea, I will uphold thee with the right hand of my righteousness."

But better than all, these very sorrows, that by nature, are mill-stones to weigh us down, become wings wherewith we fly and rejoice! "They work for us a far more exceeding and eternal weight of glory." Sanctified sorrow is one of the most effective of purifiers.

We see the legitimate effect of its ministrations in the case of Paul. He was a great sufferer. "Out of much affliction and *anguish of heart*, I wrote unto you with many tears." Bunyan and Baxter were great sufferers. It has been the rule, rather than the exception, that suffering and high sanctification have gone together.

But instead of complaining, these men of God, "were exceeding joyful in all their tribulations."

Thus, our capacity to suffer, becomes the avenue of enjoyment. The possession of eyesight makes it possible to see sights that might harrow up the soul; but, if they weep here a while, what visions await them at the right hand of God? The ear might be the inlet of weepings and wailings, and gnashings of teeth, but in heaven they will only hear the roll and swell of celestial harmonies. Thus, our very capacity to suffer, making it possible to be exceedingly happy, calls loudly for songs of grateful joy.

There, also, is our mortality. We must die. It is so appointed. The body and the soul must part. Earthly friends must be left behind. The anguish of the last hour must come.

But religion puts us in a position to welcome death as our best friend.

"I would not live alway: I ask not to stay,
Where storm after storm rises dark o'er the way;
The few lurid mornings that dawn on us here,
Are enough for life's woes, full enough for its cheer.

"Who, who would live alway; away from his God;
Away from yon heaven, that blissful abode,
Where the rivers of pleasure flow o'er the bright plains,
And the noon-tide of glory eternally reigns."

To be freed from the law of death would be an eternal imprisonment in a world of ever-recurring, ever-varying sorrow.

Hence, the hour of departure has ever been a welcome hour to God's dearest children. "Come," said one of the Janeways to the weeping friends around his dying bed—"come, see a man happier dying than you ever saw one living."

Pastor Rien, of Denmark, a little before his death, cried out, "I see the angels coming on the clouds of heaven, they are coming to take me, they descend, they stoop down, they encircle my bed, they are come to guide me to their glorious abode!"

Andrew Fuller, a half hour before his departure, opened his eyes, and with a smiling countenance, said: "Dying is sweet work, sweet work! My Father! my heavenly Father! I am looking up, I am looking up to my dear Jesus, my God! my portion! my all in all! Glory, glory! Home, home!"

Such transmutation does the King of Terrors undergo in the hands of true religion! Let one, then, but read his "title clear to mansions in the skies," and this terrible element in our nature becomes clothed with glory, and the dying saint, without presumption, may say,

"Come Death, shake hands! I'll kiss thy bands!
'Tis happiness for me to die.
What! dost thou think that I will shrink?
I'll go to immortality!"

And this immortality, so oppressive to the thought of one unprepared to die, becomes another of the choicest jewels in the Christian crown!

"So shall we be ever with the Lord!" A new and everlasting life poured through all the faculties of the soul, fear annihilated, memories so sifted as to minister only bliss, hopes and expectations fed with ever new revelations, ever new displays of divine wisdom, power and love; what a life—what a prospect!

There the soul never tires. The rest remaining for the people of God, is not the condition of repose, but the condition that results from repose; a condition not of resting, but of restedness. It is always there, as if one had just awaked from a refreshing, re-invigorating slumber. Here, if the soldier ride twenty miles to carry an order, he needs rest. There, when the glorified one has borne a message from the king to the remotest bounds of the universe, he is just as fresh for a return, as when he first spread his wings. Here, if one essay a brief meditation on the glories of God, he soon wearies. There, the spirit mounts and soars with tireless delight. Could a Humboldt, or Newton, pursue his investigations for sixty years, fresh and elastic, each succeeding hour, as at the first, what treasures of knowledge would he accumulate? There, one shall go on for ages without wearying.

Here, in the best condition, satiety will come. Power does not satisfy. Thomas Jefferson, at the end of his second presidential term, said:

"No bondsman ever put off his chains half so willingly as I these robes of office."

Riches cannot make happy. It was our lot once to walk with a friend through lawns of uncommon beauty, and to be pointed by him to a mansion in its midst, a prince might covet; from whose doors one bright morning the wealthy owner issued to find his way to a tree, upon those grounds, where he committed suicide, by hanging! His burden was satiety. With all his possessions, he could find no means of feeding hungerings and thirstings which had become intolerable.

Pleasure, too, digs her own "voluptuous tomb." Paris, the paradise of the mere pleasure-seeker, reports a larger annual number of suicides than any other city in the world.

Nothing can satisfy an immortal mind, and permanently postpone disgust and misery, but a boundless affluence of appropriate food and an everlasting affluence of variety.

Two prisoners were shut up in a cell together for years. The first year they entertained one another with stories of their lives. The second year they spoke little, for all they could say was a mere iteration and re-iteration of what had been said before. The third year was spent in almost unbroken silence. They had exhausted all their thoughts, and shut up as they were from access of any new material for thought, they could do nothing but gloomily brood in silence, and in vacuity of mind.

One shut up long in solitary confinement, at last having gazed ten thousand times upon every visible spot and angle in the walls of his cell, having ten thousand times thought over every thought, having turned over the contents of his memory until all is worn threadbare, worried and wearied with the monotony of everlasting iteration, his jaded mind goes mad!

Hence, one of the necessary conditions of tolerable, not to say happy life, in an immortal being, is an exhaustless and endlessly varying supply of objects for the employment of the mental powers.

This condition will be grandly met in the future life of the blessed in the boundlessness of the fields thrown open for exploration, and the exhaustless and ever-varying developments of divine wisdom.

Perhaps this is the significance of that river that flows from the throne of God and the Lamb. What figure more rich in suggestion of exhaustless copiousness and never-ending variety, than that of a perennial full-brimmed river. As we gaze, legions and legions of sparkling water-drops glide by, following and followed by other legions of legions, on, on, for ever, and ever, and ever.

Thus, into the ever-craving, never-cloyed mind in heaven, with never-ceasing flow, will come fresh materials for thought, study, and meditation, and as the soul looks and wonders, it will be quickened in its activities by exhilarating expectations of new and greater wonders yet to come.

Could we but mount to Abraham's side, as he sits and meditates beneath some evergreen palm on the banks of the river of life, and question him as to his past and present, and anticipated future, what a story should we hear!

All his past would be one delicious and fragrant garden of flowers. From Ur, of the Chaldees, to the grave of Macpelah, how bright every event as viewed from the heavenward side! In the darkest, cloudiest day on earth, the sun still shines in all its brightness; and could we but mount above the clouds and look down upon them, our eyes would rest upon one wide sea of glory. So, the events in the believer's life, however dark and distressing the aspect from below, looked on from heaven's battlements, are bright with all the glory of divine wisdom and love.

And from his entrance into heaven at death, to the present moment, what a poem is the story of his experience!

And as to his present, he would say, "Every object my eye lights on, increases my joy. Every sound that reaches my ear, is a note from the harmonies that roll like a boundless ocean about me. Every breeze that kisses my brow, is like the breath of Jehovah."

"But what about the future? When a boy in your father's home among the Chaldees, you little dreamed of the tears your eyes were appointed to shed, of the distress and anguish that were to wring your spirit. Now, eternity is yet before you. May there not come in the course of its evolutions and developments, experiences still less anticipated, infinitely less to be desired?"

Perhaps he would reply—

"Respecting the future, near and remote, we know nothing. Every hour brings us some new surprise. But, nestling in love of God, we experience as little anticipation of ill, as when a babe, I lay on my mother's bosom. All we know of the future, and all we desire to know, is that the source of our joys is as stable as the throne of the Redeemer."

Thus, religion, true religion brought from heaven on wings of incarnate love, beginning in the soul with faith, and repentance, and developing into loving devotion and fidelity, demonstrates its origin by its thorough and complete adaptedness to human nature. The author of this religion can be no other than the creator of the soul. This religion is the glory and crown of our nature. It is the interpreter of its profoundest mysteries. It reveals the cause of our tears, and the cure of our woes. It opens spheres of activity here, in which we take part with the angels of God. It furnishes the most effective incentives to ennobling service. Interpreting, it transmutes our very sorrows into felicities, and gives a new flavour to all our joys.

He who becomes possessor of this treasure will thank God for ever for his being, and that he was not made an angel, cherub, or seraph, but a MAN.

THE END.

www.ingramcontent.com/pod-product-compliance
Lightning Source LLC
LaVergne TN
LVHW021423110826
845150LV00007B/2051